KINGS MOUNTAIN

AND

COWPENS

KINGS MOUNTAIN

AND

COWPENS

Our Victory Was Complete

ROBERT W. BROWN JR.

THE
History
PRESS

Published by The History Press
Charleston, SC 29403
www.historypress.net

Copyright © 2009 by Robert W. Brown Jr.
All rights reserved

Images courtesy of the author unless otherwise stated.

First published 2009
Second printing 2010
Third printing 2011
Fourth printing 2012
Fifth printing 2013

ISBN 978.1.5402.2085.1

Library of Congress Cataloging-in-Publication Data

Brown, Robert W. (Robert Wilburn), 1970-
King's Mountain and Cowpens : our victory was complete / Robert W. Brown Jr.
p. cm.
Includes bibliographical references.
ISBN 978-1-59629-829-3
1. King's Mountain, Battle of, S.C., 1780. 2. Cowpens, Battle of, Cowpens, S.C., 1781. I.
Title.
E241.K5B767 2009
975.7'03--dc22
2009033686

For Jack and Thomas, may they find history as fascinating and enjoyable as I have.

CONTENTS

Preface   9
Acknowledgements   11
Introduction   13

1. The Beginning   17
2. Balance of Forces   21
3. Turning the Tide in the North   25
4. Civil War, Terrain, Weapons and Revolutionary Tactics   31
5. The South Carolina Campaign   37
6. Prelude to Kings Mountain   47
7. The Battle of Kings Mountain   63
8. Aftermath of Kings Mountain   85
9. The Winter of 1780–1781   91
10. Prelude to Cowpens   99
11. Double Envelopment at Cowpens   107
12. Aftermath of Cowpens   127
13. Race to the Dan   137
14. Conclusion   141

Notes   149
Bibliography   159

PREFACE

There have been many excellent books written about the battles of Kings Mountain and Cowpens as separate events in the American Revolution. These range from Lyman Draper's classic *Kings Mountain and Its Heroes* in the 1880s to Robert "Bert" Dunkerly's *Battle of Kings Mountain: Eyewitness Accounts* in 2007, Ed Bearss's *Battle of Cowpens* originally published in 1967 and the new standard for analyzing Cowpens: Lawrence Babits's *A Devil of a Whipping: The Battle of Cowpens* originally published in 1998. Each work brings new information and provides insights into these battles, how they were fought and what consequences they had. However there has not been a work that tied these two critical Patriot victories together. Living less than twenty miles from both fields of battle, I have often thought of the impact that these two actions had on the campaign in the South in particular and the outcome of the American Revolution as a whole. In this book I have attempted to provide an overview of and explain the connections between the two engagements and how they directly affected the course of Cornwallis's campaign in the South and his eventual surrender at Yorktown.

The work of a great many authors, historians and actual participants has been used to create this book. Legends in the field of American history such as Burke Davis, Don Higginbotham, John Gordon, John Buchanan, Lawrence Babits and Thomas Fleming have provided a solid framework on which I could build. Eyewitness accounts from Patriots, Loyalists and battlefield commanders have been used to provide the type of historical picture that only those on the scene can give us. Personal interaction with historians such as Dr. Gregory Urwin, Dr. Dan Morrill, Dennis Frye, Dr. Shepherd McKinley, Dr. James Hogue, Mr. Brian Jordan, Mr. Brandon Roos, Dr. Chris Fonvielle and Ranger Bill Troppman has given me insights for which I am eternally indebted. These individuals are consummate true believers who are passionate about their craft, and their enthusiasm has rubbed off on me.

ACKNOWLEDGEMENTS

There are far too many people who have helped and encouraged me with this work to name. I would like to thank the following people, however, and hope that I don't leave anyone out.

First I have to thank my wife, Heather Brown, for her patience while I have worked to bring this book together. Maybe one day I can make it up to her.

This book would not have been possible if a passion for reading and history had not been instilled in me from an early age. I have to credit my parents with making reading part of our routine at home: my mother modeled reading for me constantly and always encouraged me to read anything and everything.

My maternal grandmother bought me my first real history book when I was eleven years old. She may not remember buying me that book, but I do: its dog-eared pages are the seed of my knowledge of American history to this very day.

I was very fortunate to grow up with both of my grandfathers telling me vivid stories of their childhoods and adventures during the Great Depression and World War II. Unfortunately, both have long since passed away, but their storytelling is, and always will be, at the heart of my love for history.

My aunt, Ann Patterson, is owed a debt greater than I can ever repay: she has given her time and talent to turn my prepositions, dangling participles and run-on sentences into something that is readable.

ACKNOWLEDGEMENTS

Cathy Ludwig, librarian at the David Library of the American Revolution, provided copies of numerous primary and secondary sources for me. Without her diligence in looking through page after page of documents and rolls of microfilm, I wouldn't have had the sources with which to work.

John Robertson, park ranger at Cowpens National Battlefield, is perhaps the most knowledgeable individual on the Battle of Cowpens whom I have ever run across. His ideas on the battle and the thought process of Daniel Morgan helped me wrap my brain around several new ideas and gave me a clearer view of what took place on that cold January morning.

Kathy McKay, chief ranger at Cowpens National Battlefield, provided me access to John Robertson and answered numerous questions about the battle for me.

Cathy Bain, administrative assistant for Gettysburg College's Civil War Era Studies department, has always encouraged me in this project and is someone off of whom I can readily bounce ideas.

Roger Harris, principal at Crest High School, who was also my U.S. history teacher twenty years ago, encouraged me to complete this project and instilled in me a desire long ago to go above and beyond what was simply required.

I thank all of the teachers in the U.S. History Consortium, the Making of America Liberty Fellowship and the Foundations of America History Fellowship. These teachers are the elite of the history education profession and have provided me with invaluable advice and support over the years.

Ben Moore, an old friend, read through the manuscript to make sure that the story made sense to the layman.

I do need to thank my friends and entire extended family for their support and understanding. These are the people who know I am crazy and indulge my eccentricities on a daily basis.

Lastly, I want to thank all of the students whom I have been fortunate enough to teach over the past fifteen years. They are the ones who really led me down the path of wanting to write a book and made we want to know more about the subject I love. There were so many times in class that I would argue with what an author had written that one of the students would say, "Mr. Brown, why don't you just write your own book?" This work is, in many ways, the result of those comments.

INTRODUCTION

The hagiography of the American Revolution has given rise to a number of time-honored myths about the way the war was fought and eventually won. Schoolchildren, to this day, are told stories of the American Patriot taking his trusty rifle from the mantle, kissing his wife and children goodbye and going off to fight the British. The story goes that he went to win freedom, rights and independence from a despotic monarchy that was oppressing the American people. Further, this mythos states that he was high-minded and silently suffered the privations of campaigning in defense of his ideals. The story continues that he was doing this not for himself, but for his children and their children, so they could live in a democracy in which the people decided who would govern and how they would govern.

The story goes on to tell that the Americans used tactics that were unlike anything the Europeans had ever seen. The Patriots hid behind trees and fences and haystacks and fired from all manner of concealed positions. They used hit-and-run tactics that stymied the British Regular army even when the Patriots were faced with overwhelming odds. The Americans appeared from the woods, destroyed British columns and disappeared like mists in the morning sun. The American army endured the incredible hardships of the Valley Forge winter, where many starved and froze to death in the name of liberty and in defense of hearth and home.

These stories have left an indelible mark on the way we view and romanticize the American Revolution. The truth, though, does not necessarily support the myth that we have been taught to believe for more than two hundred years. This is not to say that the men who fought, suffered and eventually won American independence were not patriotic or that they endured privations that twenty-first-century students of the American Revolution can only imagine. The men and women who fought for and won independence from Great Britain were indeed great people who established a nation that has, in many ways, surpassed John Winthrop's vision of building a "City Upon a Hill."

The truth is thus: the American army was not always the steadfast group of clench-jawed men depicted in the myths. At times they fought as valiantly, if not more so, than the stories tell us, but at others they left the service at the hour of greatest danger and fled the field in the face of superior opposition. The American army also used tactics that were for the most part considered "normal" for the period. American military leaders such as George Washington and Horatio Gates had experience fighting with the British and tried to emulate their ways in order to stand toe-to-toe with them in open battle. Also, the fever of patriotism that spread among certain sects of the population around the time of the first shots also waned considerably as the war dragged on. Finally, many of the men who fought for Washington were there for the promise of land and bounties to be paid for faithful service rather than for the ideals of liberty.

All of this is not to take anything away from the astounding victory that was the American Revolution. Even through all of the mythology and hagiography that still surrounds this period of time, these people did something that no one in the world thought that they could do: they successfully gained independence, defeated or stalemated the armies the British sent into the field and created an untenable situation for the British government trying to reestablish control of the colonies. General Charles Cornwallis's band perhaps summed up the situation best when, at the formal surrender ceremony at Yorktown, they supposedly played the song "World Turned Upside Down."

The world truly did turn upside down for the British when they invaded the American South in 1779. Their campaigns through northern Georgia and South Carolina were things of military beauty to the observers of the day. But on the ridges of Kings Mountain and the plains and lowlands of Hannah's Cowpens, this campaign hit two setbacks that would ultimately prove to be fatal to the British cause in America. One battle was fought in the style eulogized in myth: Americans in buckskins and hunting shirts, using Kentucky and Pennsylvania long rifles and fighting in Indian style, destroyed a major portion of Cornwallis's Loyalist forces on the ridges of Kings

Mountain. The second was fought in brilliant military precision, combining militia, cavalry and Continental Regulars in the only successful double envelopment maneuver of the war. Both of these battles forced General Cornwallis to pursue a light and fast enemy and strike at forces that were simply beyond his reach. The result was that Cornwallis overstretched his ability to supply his ever shrinking army and made critical errors in military judgment. In the end, these two battles in the Carolinas backcountry changed the course of the war in the South and directly facilitated the demise of Cornwallis at Yorktown and the British in America.

Chapter 1
THE BEGINNING

By the spring of 1775, the American colonists had taken the unprecedented step of opening organized fire on the British regulars sent to Lexington and Concord in Massachusetts. This step launched a war that in the end would forge a nation out of thirteen individual colonies. Even as those shots were fired on the village green in Lexington and at the North Bridge in Concord, few believed that they were firing the first shots in a war for independence, because at their very core Americans were British. They believed that they were fighting to maintain their rights as Englishmen and to preserve their unique place in the British Empire. The status quo prior to the French and Indian War was what most people in the colonies desired, not the radical idea of formal separation and independence.

American colonial militia, some erroneously known as "minutemen," had been authorized by the First Continental Congress to defend against military emergencies that could arise from the British regulars stationed in the various colonies. These very militia units converged on Boston, where the British regulars had retreated. Within a short period of time, they had the city surrounded and commanded the hills ringing the city. This army, contemptuously called "rabble" by the regulars, had embarked on a journey that would see fighting in every colony, in Canada and on the high seas. Eventually, the war would spread and become an international affair as Britain's enemies availed themselves of the opportunity to weaken their old colonial rival. What began as a desperate attempt to protect their rights, as the colonists saw them at least, would end with the formation of a new nation.

That army of farmers and men who saw themselves as Patriots was about to engage the most feared military force in the world in a pitched battle on the outskirts of Boston. Few learned people and military minds of the day believed that the Americans could stand up to the combined might of the British regulars arrayed in battle, bayonets fixed, charging and firing en masse. Most believed that the Americans had won the skirmish at and beyond Concord because the British were not there in force and that they had not been expecting armed resistance. This same line of thought also said that the so-called Patriots would scatter as chaff to the breeze at the sight of the regulars and their bayonets gleaming in the sun. These people could not have been more wrong.

As the world watched, the British regulars came out of Boston to offer battle to the newly christened Continental army on the eminence of Breed's Hill (erroneously called Bunker Hill for posterity). The Continentals held the most crucial of military advantages, the high ground, and the regulars paid an extreme price as a result. Time and again the British regulars charged up the long slope, and each time they were repulsed with appalling casualties. It is here that Patriot Major William Prescott supposedly told his men "Don't fire until you see the whites of their eyes." The regulars charged the American positions twice without appreciable effect. Finally, the commander of the regulars, General William Howe, rallied his troops and charged one final time. This charge carried into the American earthworks and evolved into savage hand-to-hand combat. The Americans were running so low on ammunition that they were eventually forced to abandon their position. The British had succeeded in taking the position, but were unable to disband the American army that had the city surrounded.

Even though the battle on Breed's Hill was a tactical defeat for the Continental army, it was a strategic victory for the American cause. The exertions of the Continental army on the heights around Charlestown and Boston demonstrated to the rest of the country and the world that the Americans could indeed fight effectively. The Continental Congress had recently named George Washington as the army's commander, and the southern colonies had tacitly agreed to join in the conflict. Finally, the battle ended all hope of a reconciliation and return to the status quo even though the so-called Olive Branch Petition was sent to England asking for a return to peaceful relations.

The following months saw Washington move to tighten his virtual siege of the city of Boston and the British garrison. As his lines moved closer and closer, the British sensed the precariousness of their situation and withdrew their forces by sea. The opening act of the American Revolution drew to a close, and it seemed that the colonies were well on their way to establishing home rule if not outright independence.

Unfortunately, the year 1776 began a dark period for the Continental army. The British menaced the important port of New York, and Washington shifted his army to meet the threat. In doing so, Washington demonstrated that he was still learning on the job and made the crucial mistake of dividing his meager forces in the face of a superior enemy. The result was that New York was lost, and Washington's army was chased through New Jersey and into Pennsylvania. To make matters worse, Washington's army was literally disintegrating because the soldiers' terms of enlistment were expiring. Only the daring attack on Trenton over the Christmas holiday gave rise to Patriot hopes as the year closed.

Even through the military reversals experienced by Washington's army, the Continental Congress took the incredible step of issuing the now famous Declaration of Independence. In this monumental document, chief author Thomas Jefferson laid the foundation for the American nation. He espoused the idea that all people have inalienable rights (which John Locke called natural rights)—life, liberty and the pursuit of happiness—and that the legitimate function of government was to secure these rights for the people. He further argued that governments derived their powers from the consent of the governed and that when a government becomes destructive to either inalienable rights or consent of the governed that it is "the Right of the People to alter or to abolish it." Jefferson went on to provide a list of grievances to show the nation and even the other nations of the world why the American colonies were taking such a leap into the great unknown of independence. While the Declaration of Independence did not have an immediate impact on the war itself, it did provide a formal break with Great Britain and called to light the reasons for this separation. Unfortunately, the Americans were not of one opinion in terms of independence or how to achieve it.

Chapter 2
BALANCE OF FORCES

As the American Revolution began a new and arduous phase, the balance of forces was telling. On paper the insurrection should have been short work for the British Empire. There were two key advantages that the British had over the Americans: manpower and resources. Dr. Dan Morrill, a history professor at the University of North Carolina–Charlotte, has often stated, "Amateurs talk about strategy and tactics, professionals talk about logistics." With this in mind, it would seem that with the overwhelming manpower and resource advantages at its disposal that the British should have won the conflict without breaking so much as a sweat.

In terms of military power, the British were able to count more than 270 warships to prowl the waters of the Americas and beyond, whereas America had to create a navy from scratch. The British army was built to take on the most powerful nations of Europe and mustered more than fifty thousand well-trained men in 1775. The Continental army was composed of men whose enlistments ran out at one-year intervals and never was able to put much more than about twenty thousand men into the field at any given time. When the Continental army was able to muster a sizeable force, much of it was militia, men who served locally and were apt to leave the service without a moment's notice. This unreliability made the militia unpopular with many Continental officers but was necessary if the Americans were to fight the British with anything near equal numbers.[1]

The British also had a huge advantage in terms of population from which to draw manpower. The population of Great Britain in 1775 was roughly 8 million people compared to the colonial population of roughly 2.5 million. Based on simple arithmetic, the British would seem to have an overwhelming advantage, but it was greater than even the numbers would make it seem. Of the 2.5 million total Americans, about 500,000 were slaves and were officially excluded from the Continental army at the beginning of the war and local militias. There were an estimated 400,000 to 500,000 Americans who were Loyalists, with nearly 50,000 serving in the British army at one point or another during the war. Also, there was a large percentage of Americans who were simply neutral. All in all, the British had about a six-to-one population advantage during the American Revolution.[2]

Economically, Great Britain was the cradle of the Industrial Revolution and, at the time of the American Revolution, was the most industrialized nation in the world. Great Britain had heavy industry, shipbuilding, precious metals, a functioning and powerful economy and agriculture in abundance. America, on the other hand, had little industry and had to attempt to create an economy amid a war. This handicap led America to look abroad for supplies and caused almost disastrous runaway inflation during the war.[3]

While the population and military manpower figures look impressive for the British, they do not tell the entire story. In order to subdue the colonies and pacify the areas captured, the British high command estimated that about fifty thousand troops would be needed at all times. It was virtually impossible for the British to concentrate this number of troops in the colonies because of commitments elsewhere such as the Indies and India. One solution that the British tried was to hire mercenaries from the German princes to help prosecute the war. These "Hessians," so named for the German state of Hess, were seen as a slap in the face by Americans as foreigners sent by the Crown and Parliament to subjugate them. Even with increased attempts at recruiting and the hiring of the Hessians, attrition from fighting, diseases and associated issues meant that the British army in America never approached the level the high command believed they needed to successfully subdue the rebellion.

Geography was also a problem for the British. The so-called mother country lay an ocean away, making it extremely difficult to stage military operations and rotate units in the field. Even with a navy that was able to secure the oceans and coastline, once the British moved inland, it became harder to control the countryside. In Europe, there were primary military objectives that armies attacked and defended as a matter of course. These included industrial centers, capitals and large cities. In America there was no supremely vital political, population or industrial center to take. For example, when the British captured Philadelphia during the war, the Congress simply packed up and moved elsewhere. Add to this the scattered nature of the American population, and geography truly worked against the British.[4]

To make matters worse, the British also were very arrogant toward the Americans. The high command, almost without fail, made one of the most critical errors that any military establishment can make: underestimating the enemy. The British felt that the Continental army could be frightened into surrendering and that the hardened regulars and Hessians could defeat any army that the Americans brought into the field. This arrogance created opportunities for the Continental army that helped turn the tide of the war and either reverse British or maintain American momentum. At places such as Bunker Hill, Trenton, Saratoga, Kings Mountain, Cowpens and Guilford Court House, this British arrogance would lead to their undoing.

Chapter 3

TURNING THE TIDE
IN THE NORTH

In 1777, the British adopted a strategy designed to split New York in half and cut off New England from the rest of America. By splitting the colonies, it was thought that it would be easier to subjugate New England and bring the war to a close. To accomplish this end, General John Burgoyne was to move his army southward from Canada, and General William Howe was to move northward from New York. As with the best-laid plans, these went awry as soon as they were put into place.

General Burgoyne recaptured Fort Ticonderoga in New York and continued to move south toward the point where the armies were scheduled to link up. Burgoyne's army was harassed by New England militia and even Native Americans, who felled trees, burned bridges and did everything in their power to disrupt his progress. Howe, comfortable in New York City, analyzed the plan and belatedly found a fatal flaw. If he packed up his army and left New York, Washington's force in New Jersey would be able to reoccupy the town, which would be a major political coup for the Americans. Also, General Howe was having a very pleasant time in New York, enjoying the company of a woman, who was not his wife, and failed to advance and link up with Burgoyne.

The commander of the American northern army, Horatio Gates, spent a great deal of energy setting up defenses in the New York interior to deal with Burgoyne's threat. Using the natural terrain to his advantage, Gates established powerful defensive works on Bemis Heights. The cannons ensconced in these positions commanded the river and land approaches to the area and would make it costly for the British to assault directly. The existence of the position would leave the British in a military quandary. If the British tried to flank the position from the east, they would have to go well out of their way and lose the element of surprise because the roads could not support an army moving in force. The river guarded the western approaches, and the Americans were positioned on commanding high ground.

In September 1777, Burgoyne's army reached Freeman's Farm near the village of Saratoga, New York. His eight-thousand-man army was met by about ten thousand Americans led by General Horatio Gates. One of Gates's lieutenants was Colonel Daniel Morgan, who commanded a corps of about five hundred light infantry, skilled in the use of the rifle and utilizing tactics not common on the European or American battlefields of the day. Morgan had initially been sent north by George Washington to keep an eye on Howe and Burgoyne and to harass the Indian allies of the British.[5] Morgan's men were so effective at their work that the Indians, on whom the British relied to instill terror in the populace and provide intelligence on the whereabouts of the American army, vanished from the scene.

Daniel Morgan was born in 1736 in New Jersey (there are claims by Pennsylvania as well) but ran away from home when he was seventeen. Morgan ended up in Virginia, where be began a life of wagoning and brawling. Morgan was a physical specimen, especially for the day, standing six feet tall with broad shoulders and large arms. Being a wagoner brought Morgan into contact with British general Edward Braddock during his ill-fated campaign against the French at Fort Duquesne during the French and Indian War. Braddock had impressed all of the transportation in western Virginia to help in his march, and Morgan was compelled to go along. Part of Morgan's duties was to transport supplies to Fort Chiswell in western Virginia.

During the expedition, Morgan showed his fiery temper when a British officer insulted him and struck him with the flat of a sword. Morgan struck the offending officer with his fist and knocked him to the ground. A court-martial convicted Morgan and sentenced him to 500 lashes. Morgan claimed his entire life that he remained conscious during this brutal beating. He also claimed that the British only gave him 499 lashes; he knew, he said, because he counted every one of them. In years to come, Morgan would tell the story over and over again, and when he wanted to get the attention of his soldiers, he would strip to the waist and show them the scars left by the British whip. After the debacle at Fort Duquense, Morgan eventually enlisted in the Virginia Rangers under the command of George Washington. At one point during his service with the Rangers, he was scouting on the western Virginia frontier when Morgan and a companion were ambushed by Indians. Morgan received a bullet in his cheek that left a visible scar and took out a number of teeth.

After the war, Morgan settled down in the lower Shenandoah Valley near modern Winchester and became one of the most respected men in the community. He married, built a fine home and raised a family during these years. When the Revolution began, Morgan was given command of one of the two regiments of Virginia riflemen. He was at Boston with Washington during the siege and was later sent to Canada with Benedict Arnold. In Canada, he was captured at the Battle of Quebec in 1775. He was paroled and waited at home in Virginia to be exchanged, and in 1777 he joined Washington's army again before Washington sent him north with Horatio Gates.

On Freeman's Farm near the sleepy village of Saratoga, Morgan and his light infantry met the lead elements of Burgoyne's army. Morgan deployed his men in the forested area near the farm, where the American rifle tactics could be brought to bear and the British superiority in artillery and use of the bayonet would be negated.[6] During this part of the engagement, the fighting was incredibly violent, and each side captured the field more than once on that fateful September day. Burgoyne ordered more of his soldiers to the field to reinforce the lead elements as the battle raged. In doing so, he significantly outnumbered the riflemen under Morgan, who prudently retired from the field. Even though the British held the actual field of battle, they were unable to move any farther because they did not know what forces Gates had in the vicinity. As a result of this lack of military intelligence, Burgoyne ordered his men to adopt a defensive position, and they awaited reinforcements from New York. The expected reinforcements actually moved out of New York but turned back after General Howe again feared for the city's safety.[7]

In the meantime, Burgoyne's army was slowly wasting away. They had been on slim rations since the engagement at Freeman's Farm, and winter was fast approaching upstate New York. In early October, Burgoyne sent out a group of soldiers, complete with cannons, to probe and bombard the American lines and gather food and forage for the rest of the army. The Americans attacked this small British force and compelled them to retreat back into their own entrenchments. Gates correctly sensed that the time was now right to attack the British in their weakened state. Gates had gathered an army of about thirteen thousand men of all arms and set about to encircle the British and bring them to battle.

The Americans attacked at a crucial point in the British defenses and succeeded in carrying a position that let them get in behind the British lines. This collapse of these defensive works forced the British back into a last-ditch defensive line near the Hudson River. Burgoyne, knowing the danger his army was in, began a hasty and hazardous retreat toward the north. His tired, hungry and ragged army tried to escape the American force they thought was pursuing them. The American army utilized the light and fast militia to get ahead of Burgoyne's retreat and block them near Saratoga, while the rest of the army finished encircling them. After being surrounded, Burgoyne surrendered to Gates on October 17, 1777.[8]

The Battle of Saratoga had a major impact on the war as it turned the tide of the war in the North in favor of the Americans. After word of the British defeat reached Europe, Britain's old rival France agreed to an alliance with America. France would provide loans, arms, munitions and, more importantly, troops and a fleet to help prosecute the war. French intervention was not based on the high-minded belief that the American colonies should form a separate nation built on the ideas of liberty and natural rights, but rather as a means to weaken Great Britain and exact a measure of revenge for its humiliating defeat in the Seven Years' (French and Indian) War.

General Horatio Gates received many accolades for defeating the British at Saratoga. In fact many in Congress were so enamored of Gates that there was a movement in Philadelphia to remove George Washington and replace him with Gates. Though this movement never made much headway, Gates was destined to play a critical role later in the war. Daniel Morgan, on the other hand, felt slighted by the attention given Gates. He rightfully felt that his own contributions to the battle had played a crucial role in the victory, yet he had been overlooked for promotion to brigadier general. In a moment of injured pride, Morgan returned home to Winchester, Virginia, and left the army for a time.[9] Gates was subsequently sent to the southern colonies to take command of the southern army and stop the British offensive in the area.

The year 1777 would also see a major transformation of Washington's army. Encamped in Valley Forge, Pennsylvania, Washington's army fought the cold of winter and pangs of hunger as they waited for the spring campaign season. As with many aspects of the American Revolution, myth has taken the place of fact when it comes to the Valley Forge winter. Contrary to Revolutionary mythology, no soldier froze or starved to death during that long, bleak winter. Poetically situated between Mount Misery and Mount Hope, Washington's army was forged into a force that could stand up to the

Turning the Tide in the North

British in the open field. Prussian drillmaster Baron Frederich von Steuben, who was neither a baron nor a field marshal, drilled the Continental army into a fighting force that could stand up to the British in an open fight. Von Steuben's European techniques and attention to detail created an army of soldiers that could successfully fight in the traditional military manner of the day. By the springtime, Washington had a force that could rightfully be called an army.[10]

A series of battles over the next year, including Monmouth Court House, showed the British that the Americans were a force to be reckoned with. No longer could the British regulars and Hessians show up on the field and know that the Continental army would break and run. For both sides, the war entered a new phase in the North, one in which neither side could gain a clear advantage. Both sides were content to maneuver and skirmish as the focus of the war shifted to other theatres and abortive attempts at peace.

As the year 1780 dawned, the war was at a stalemate in the North. The British population grew weary of the conflict, and the British government tried to settle the war peacefully. The so-called Carlisle Commission ended up being a failure at settling the war, but the British were able to gather a bit of what they thought was valuable intelligence. The British were told that the southern colonies Georgia, South Carolina, North Carolina and Virginia contained a large number of Loyalists and that they would rally to the Crown if the British government showed interest in occupying the colonies.

The British were victims of hearing what they wanted to hear from the Loyalists at the Carlisle Commission. In the North, British experience had been that the Loyalists lay low and only rallied around king and country when the British army was in the vicinity. Even with this knowledge, the British high command believed that if they landed an army in the American South, the Loyalists would be so emboldened that they would rise up and bring the colonies back into the imperial fold.

Chapter y
CIVIL WAR, TERRAIN, WEAPONS AND REVOLUTIONARY TACTICS

When one hears or reads the term "civil war," especially in an American context, they almost immediately think of the years 1861–65. While the American Civil War of that period was most certainly a civil war, America's first war between elements of its own population began during the American Revolution. As previously discussed, not all Americans were Patriots who wanted to break away from Britain. This led to a war not only between the Patriots and the British but also between the Patriots and the Loyalists (or Tories) and between local families and alliances in the backcountry. This was a war that would evolve into a period of backcountry anarchy that would not be seen again until the infamous "Bleeding Kansas" period in the late 1850s.

The war brought out long-held animosities that bubbled to the surface as the conflict moved to and fro. In North Carolina and South Carolina, there was considerable east-versus-west conflict in both colonies prior to the outbreak of the Revolution. The upstate gentry in both areas were jealous and fearful of the power and perceived tyranny of the Lowcountry elites. Add to this volatile situation a series of Indian wars, British occupation and perceived slights, and it made for potential anarchy. The arrival of armies foraging and plundering the countryside was the spark that ignited the tinder of the Carolinas backcountry.

Families were split along political lines, with members actually engaging one another on the field of battle. Even Benjamin Franklin, arch-Patriot, would see his own son disavow America and independence and live estranged from his family after the war. In William Gilmore Simms's book, *The Scout*, Simms might have laid out these feelings best when he wrote "A man's best friend now-a-days is…his rifle."[11] This statement seems very ominous in the twenty-first century, but to the men and women who lived in the Carolinas backcountry of the eighteenth century it was in many ways the truth. People who were unfortunate enough to live in the path of the warring armies were caught in a dangerous predicament of where their loyalties lay.

The changing fortunes of war brought about shifts in the loyalties of the people. Wherever the British army was in control, the Loyalists would rally around. When this happened, there were reprisals and revenge on the minds of the Loyalists who had been dealt with harshly by the Patriots. For others there was the opportunity to enrich themselves at their neighbors' expense and profit from a war that appeared to be going well for the British. However, as soon as the British army moved on as the needs of the campaign dictated, the Patriots would see that the Loyalists reaped the whirlwind that they had sowed. Shootings, whippings, arson, fistfights and theft were unfortunately all too common during this period.

One story of reprisal in particular is worth noting. Thomas Brown was a successful farmer near Augusta, Georgia. A group of so-called Patriots paid the well-known planter a visit at his farm, demanding that he sign an oath supporting independence. When Brown asked that he be able to live by his own convictions without being molested, the Patriots responded with the worst sort of assault. Brown was bound and beaten, and parts of his body were dipped in hot tar and placed over a fire. The resultant heat caused Brown's foot to catch fire and scarred it for the remainder of his life. It is very easy to understand the hatred that Brown had for Patriots and the independence movement and why he became a Loyalist militia leader.

Far too many people, from history buffs to professional historians, rely on two-dimensional history as a base for their analyses and conclusions. Their conclusions are rooted in the black-and-white images on paper that transform themselves in the mind's eye into a personal view of the field. Unfortunately, the lines and drawings on maps in books, magazines and pamphlets provide us with a very stilted and limited idea of the topographical forces that shaped the various battles throughout history. In order to truly understand how and why a battle unfolded the way that it did, you have to get out and walk the field—and not simply walk a paved trail and read a few interpretive markers; you have to walk the field and see it from the perspective of the combatants of both sides with an educated eye toward the terrain and tactics of the time.

Civil War, Terrain, Weapons and Revolutionary Tactics

National Park Service historian Robert "Bert" Dunkerly, in his excellent *Kings Mountain Walking Tour Guide*, urges readers to use the U.S. military mnemonic of KOCOA.[12] This stands for Key terrain; Obstacles; Cover; Observation and fields of fire; and Avenues of approach and retreat. While these concepts are crucial to the military art, they can be overwhelming for even the best-trained historians as they attempt to study a given battle or campaign. Civil War and National Park Service historian Dennis Frye of Harpers Ferry National Historical Park has broken KOCOA down to three crucial points that provide the enthusiast and historian alike with an accurate way to view a battlefield. The first point is three simple words: terrain, terrain and terrain.[13] The terrain is the key to any battlefield, no matter what the conflict or its location. The second point is that the high ground is almost always superior to lower-lying areas. The third point is that the military crest of any high ground is different from the geographic crest and that knowing and using this difference can greatly alter the outcome of a given battle. Using these three salient points, one can view any battlefield with some degree of accuracy and in a fashion that no book or other two-dimensional representation can match.

One supposed maxim of warfare, especially eighteenth-century warfare, is that being on the defensive is usually easier than being on the offensive. Being on the defensive usually means that you have the choice of terrain and have improved it in some fashion to make it more formidable. This improvement can be anything from stacking logs and limbs up to form crude breastworks to actually digging rifle pits and trench systems. The attacker must then assail these works while coming under fire from the defenders, all of which makes it a grim task at best. With this in mind, an attacker generally needs a two-and-a-half-to-one advantage in manpower in order to ensure success in an attack against a prepared enemy who is on the defensive.[14]

Lastly, there is a definite psychology to battle that is eerily similar to that in modern sports such as football. In the game of football, there is something commentators and fans refer to as momentum. A team with momentum experiences success on the field, and that success tends to breed more success and good fortune. In football, a team intercepting a pass from the opposing quarterback and returning the interception for a touchdown in a close game can swing momentum to its side. In the resulting series, the team tends to play better and feeds off that success. In warfare, again especially eighteenth-century warfare, there was a unique brand of momentum, as well. In the case of the defenders, if an attack was beaten back soundly and with heavy loss, then it was likely that future attacks would meet the same end (all things being equal). On the attacking side, there was a similar situation, if an attack or a portion of an attack gained a breakthrough at any point, then it was easier for other breakthroughs to follow in rapid succession.[15]

While these loosely defined "rules" of the battlefield applied in most Revolutionary War engagements, you will see that the fight on the ridges of Kings Mountain is the exception that helps prove the rule and that the battle at Hannah's Cowpens is the very archetype of that rule.

The weaponry used in the Revolution was as wide-ranging and varied as the war itself. Soldiers used firearms, artillery and edged weapons such as knives and swords, and there were even some reports of men wearing forms of armor. However, shoulder-fired weapons were the most common and deadliest on the far-flung battlefields. From Lexington and Concord to Yorktown, the shoulder-fired weapon was the implement that was crucial in deciding the outcome. Artillery, bayonets and other weapons had their moments, but the shoulder-fired weapon was the queen of the eighteenth-century battlefield.

The shoulder-fired weapons in the Revolution fell into two main categories: rifles and muskets. The differences between these two types of weapons were many and provided the respective strengths and weaknesses that affected their use on the battlefield. The rifle was first and foremost a hunting weapon. The men of the backcountry used their rifles to hunt game and put food on the table for their families. Since they had to be carried over great distances, these weapons were made to be as light as possible. The barrels of the weapons had a series of spiral grooves cut into them. When a round was fired, the ball was grabbed by the grooves, and as it was pushed through the barrel, it imparted a spin on the ball. This spin stabilized the flight of the bullet and increased its accuracy. In fact, there are stories of backwoodsmen hunting squirrels with these rifles and being so accurate that they could pass a bullet between a squirrel's chin and chest. This close shave would create a concussion wave that would stop the squirrel's heart and wouldn't harm any of the meat. In the hands of a skilled marksman, a rifle was an extremely deadly weapon out to several hundreds of yards. If one of these crack shots got a man-sized target in his sights, the odds were that they would hit it and hit it exactly where they intended.

The very characteristics that made the rifle so deadly also made it somewhat unsuitable for the eighteenth-century battlefield. The light weight of the weapon meant that it was not very effective in close quarters combat. If used as a club or blunt-force weapon, the stock was prone to crack, rendering the weapon useless. The grooves that engaged the bullet and imparted spin made the weapon slow to reload since the round had to literally be rammed down the barrel along with a greased patch. After firing a few rounds, the barrel and rifling grooves would get fouled by unburned powder and residue, which required the soldier to clean the weapon before it could be used again—a daunting prospect on a hotly contested battlefield.

The smoothbore musket was the typical weapon for the major armies of the world at that time. A musket was significantly shorter than a rifle and was heavier, making it excel in close quarters combat. In addition, the musket had a bayonet lug on the barrel that would allow a soldier to mount a three-sided bayonet for use in combat. The bayonet was a terror weapon, and brandishing it on the battlefield tested the mettle of even the most veteran troops. The musket was a smoothbore weapon, meaning that the barrel did not have the grooves of a rifle. As a result of the smooth bore, the musket was far less accurate than the rifle, having an effective range of well under eighty yards.

Even though it wasn't very accurate, the smooth bore allowed for much faster loading and firing of the musket than what you could get with a rifle. A well-trained soldier could get off up to a minimum of three rounds per minute from a musket, whereas a soldier armed with a rifle would be lucky to fire two shots in the same time. By massing soldiers in ranks and firing in volleys, an army armed with muskets would be able to put a staggering amount of hot lead in the air at any one time. Another key feature of the musket was that it did not suffer from the fouling issues that plagued the rifle, making it a much more reliable weapon on the battlefield.

Both rifles and muskets used a flint to strike a steel plate that produced a strong spark to ignite the powder charge. The flints used during the American Revolution had a serviceable life of roughly sixteen shots and had to be replaced. While a soldier could carry upward of fifty rounds of ammunition, he would have to replace his flint a number of times during the battle, possibly while under fire from the enemy.

The differences between the two types of shoulder-fired weapons caused tactics to evolve that suited their use. Officers such as Daniel Morgan understood that a unit armed with rifles could play a crucial role on the eighteenth-century battlefield. Their tactics would be such that they would not engage the enemy at close range or in close quarters combat but would use well-aimed fire to inflict as much damage as possible from the fewest number of men. Morgan's force in particular became an elite unit within the American army and was used to great effect by General Washington and later General Horatio Gates. Even with Morgan's startling successes, units of true riflemen were a distinct minority in the American army. The British regulars and Hessians relied on the massed, and impressive, firepower of the musket on the battlefield. Their tactics were the dressed ranks, standing shoulder to shoulder, and firing on a given command. The sheer weight and volume of fire was meant to inflict damage en masse on the enemy's similarly arrayed lines of battle. In an infantry-versus-infantry engagement, both sides would exchange volleys, and when one side gained the upper hand, they would charge with fixed bayonets.

As with most things about the Revolution, there is a set of myths surrounding the weapons used in the war that does the participants a great disservice. The great myth says that the Patriot forces were armed with their trusty hunting rifles, while the British and their Hessian hirelings were armed with the Brown Bess musket. This simply is not true. George Washington set out to create an army that could stand toe-to-toe with the best that the British could send against them. In order to do this, he armed his men with weapons similar to the British. This included captured Brown Bess muskets, as well as excellent French-made weapons. The battles that Washington fought against the British, especially after the Valley Forge winter, were in the European style with roughly equivalent weapons.

In the Carolinas backcountry, the story was a bit different. In the South, there was a great deal of local and state militia activity, and the militia generally armed themselves with whatever firearms they had available. This means that many of the skirmishes and pitched battles fought from Charleston on through to Yorktown had a great many rifle-versus-musket engagements. Patriot leaders such as Francis Marion, Thomas Sumter, Charles Campbell and Andrew Pickens had large numbers of men who were armed with their hunting rifles, with which they were intimately familiar. These skirmishes and battles would serve as the core of many of the half-truths about the Revolution that have been handed down from generation to generation. These lesser-known engagements would also help seal the end of Britain's dominion over the thirteen colonies and facilitate the birth of the United States of America.

The tactics employed in the Carolina backcountry typically matched the weaponry of the combatants. The British army, however, tended to follow the prescribed European model in the major engagements of the campaign. In battles such as Kings Mountain, the Patriot militia would indeed engage in partisan tactics of using extreme cover, directing carefully aimed fire, ambushes and avoidance of a toe-to-toe fight until the last moment. The Carolinas would see some of the most diverse types of fighting in the American Revolution and ultimately would decide the outcome of the war.

Chapter 5
THE SOUTH CAROLINA CAMPAIGN

In the late winter of 1780, a British force of more than 9,000 men commanded by General Sir Henry Clinton was landed near Charleston, South Carolina. Massachusetts-born General Benjamin Lincoln was charged with its defense and was promised 3,000 reinforcements by the Continental Congress. Only 750 were sent, and they arrived too late to help in the defense of the port city. The British laid siege to the city and eventually forced its surrender along with its sizable garrison of the Continental army. The only significant field army between Savannah and the Potomac River had essentially been taken off of the table. The only force standing in the way of the British were local militia groups, who often fought as much with one another as they had the British, and the reinforcements that Congress had belatedly sent. The Continental reinforcements would form the core of the army that would defend South Carolina against Cornwallis's troops. General Lincoln's men were eventually condemned to the prison hulks, old warships with their masts cut away and permanently anchored in New York Harbor, where many would die of disease, exposure to heat and cold, malnutrition and extreme cruelty by their captors. Shortly after the fall of Charleston, General Clinton would return to New York, and his second in command, General Charles the Earl Cornwallis, would take over.

During the early summer of 1780, Cornwallis's army moved into the interior of South Carolina. It looked as if the information they had received during the Carlisle Commission was at least tacitly true, and the southern colonies would be easy to return to the imperial fold. By the end of May, his army had begun using the area around Camden as a base of operations. One prize had eluded Cornwallis's army, though: the Patriot governor of South Carolina, John Rutledge, was trying to escape. The only organized regular fighting force still in South Carolina was Colonel Abraham Buford's Virginia regiment and a few of Lieutenant Colonel William Washington's dragoons. Buford's men retreated slowly through South Carolina, fending off the British and screening governor Rutledge from capture until he could reach North Carolina and safety. Cornwallis sent the headstrong Banastre Tarleton with a mixed force of cavalry and light infantry, soon to be commonly known as Tarleton's Legion, to pursue Buford and bring the governor to ground. Eventually, Rutledge would separate from Buford's men and make it to the north state, and from there events get fuzzy in terms of the fate of Buford's men.

Banastre Tarleton was born to relatively wealthy parents in Liverpool in 1754. When he came of age, Tarleton studied law at Oxford but would rather have been riding horses and involved in other athletic pursuits. By all accounts, Tarleton was a relatively short, stocky man who was thick-shouldered, strong and athletic. These attributes would serve him well during his campaigns in America.

While at Oxford, Tarleton gambled away the family fortune and finally decided on a career in the army. He was able to purchase an officership in the First Regiment Dragoons and embarked on a military career. Seeking action and adventure, Tarleton sailed to America at the beginning of the war. In the northern campaign, Tarleton advanced through his deeds and actions rather than through family connections. Tarleton was perhaps best known in the British army for the way that he used a combined force of cavalry and light infantry, forming them into a formidable fighting force that performed excellent service. Unfortunately, Tarleton's name would become synonymous with brutality in the South Carolina campaign.

There are two general accounts of what happened at the Waxhaws to Buford and his men at the hands of Tarleton's men in what would become known as Buford's Massacre. One states that Buford determined that he could no longer keep Tarleton at bay and decided to ask for terms of surrender, sending out a flag of truce. As Tarleton tried to accept the flag of truce, he was fired upon and his horse was shot out from under him. As Tarleton went down, his men believed that he was killed, and they exacted their revenge on Buford's men, killing and hacking those trying to surrender. The other account is much more sinister, stating that Tarleton offered Buford's men quarter, and when the colonials' arms were stacked, the British attacked the unarmed men. No matter what actually happened, Buford's command lost over four hundred men, many to multiple saber and bayonet wounds. Patriots would raise the cry of "Buford's Quarter" when dealing with British prisoners or British soldiers trying to surrender. Banastre Tarleton gained the nom de guerre of "Bloody Ban" or "Bloody Benny." Patriot militia leaders used this episode to recruit new soldiers to defend the area against the onslaught of Cornwallis and Tarleton.

Up to this point, the British thought that the process of reclaiming South Carolina for the Crown had been going well.[16] However, the way the British attempted to administer government in the colony left a lot to be desired. The British attempted to make the citizens take an oath of loyalty to the Crown and followed up that insult with the requirement that they be ready to fight in support of the mother country. As would be expected, this policy led to a great deal of dissent among a population that had already been split along the lines of Patriot or Loyalist leanings. It also created further fuel for Patriot militia leaders to recruit new soldiers and caused hardship for those Loyalists trying to organize their own militia. The backcountry had become an area ripe with reprisal and villainy, and the British policies only added to that situation. In areas where Loyalists controlled the countryside, there was considerable pillaging of Patriot property and abuse of Patriots and their families.

The summer of 1780 saw many violent engagements in the South Carolina backcountry as Cornwallis's army continued its march northward toward North Carolina. These engagements would soon show the British that reclaiming the south for the Empire would not be nearly as easy as it had seemed in the spring. In fighting at Williamson's Plantation in July, an American Loyalist officer who fought with Tarelton, Captain Christian Huck, was ambushed and killed by a force of Patriot militia. This battle, known as the Battle of Huck's Defeat, is indicative of the nature of the fighting in the Carolinas at the time. Huck and his men had been sent to secure the area and help support the officials administering the British loyalty oath. Huck and his unit had, in the process of intimidating the locals, confiscated property and abused a great many people.[17] In fact, Huck had taken several men prisoner whom he planned to hang for treason. As would happen often in the backcountry, the Patriots rose up and attacked the Loyalists under Huck, with Huck being killed in the attack. Only a small number of Huck's men would escape the onslaught of the aroused local militia. The pattern would become familiar to the British in the Carolinas: when antagonized, the local militia would appear and inflict casualties, and even defeats, on small detachments;

then they would disappear before the main army could be brought to bear. This war was to be a bloody and nasty affair where the rules of civilized warfare were practiced irregularly, if they were practiced at all.

From the outside, the southern colonies indeed seemed ripe for the British to take over. One rumor making its rounds was that the Continental Congress would give up Georgia and South Carolina to Britain in exchange for an end to hostilities. While not true, the Congress responded with a declaration stating that they would indeed fight for South Carolina and not simply turn it over as a prize of war. In order to forestall the British from running rampant through South Carolina, General Horatio Gates, the hero of Saratoga, was sent to South Carolina to whip an army into shape and stop the British from gaining control of the South. George Washington was not in agreement with Gates's selection, instead backing Nathanael Greene to be the commander of the Southern army. Washington's star was dim at this point of the Revolution, and his advice and suggestions were not heeded in this matter.

From the very beginning of his command in the southern department, Gates made error after error in judgment. At his disposal was a ragtag army of roughly 1,500 Continental troops, including the reinforcements bound for Charleston, and about the same number of militia, a force that compared to Cornwallis's field army. When Gates arrived in South Carolina, he lamented that he had an army without strength and a war chest without treasure. Gates's first error was marching his men through a barren area of South Carolina where there were virtually no supplies and very little forage. His men lived for weeks on what they could scrounge from the countryside, mainly green apples and wild onions. "The army soon felt the scarcity of provisions; and their fatigue, fasting and repeated disappointments as to supplies so exasperated them, that their murmurs became very audible."[18] As a result of this logistical nightmare, Gates's men were physically exhausted, and many were ill when the time came to face the enemy. The second major error that Gates committed was viewing his Carolina and Georgia militia in the same light as the riflemen under Morgan who had served with him in the North. The local militia groups in the South were not trained like Continental regulars and could not have been expected to respond like regulars when the battle commenced. Before Gates's army ever saw the first British soldier, dragoon or Hessian jaeger, the battle was lost.

General Gates marched his little army toward the British, who were marching into the South Carolina countryside. Gates intended to surprise and attack General Cornwallis at or near Camden. Unknown to Gates,

The South Carolina Campaign

Cornwallis had already arrived at Camden and had plans to attack Gates's army that was encamped nearby. Both armies sent out scouting parties on the evening of August 15, and they came into contact with each other in the woods and opened fire. This brisk engagement showed each army where the other was and what the intentions of each were.

The battlefield at Camden was interesting in terms of terrain. There was no commanding high ground to speak of, so neither side gained a true advantage there. The area was swampy, and the British army formed its lines in such a way that both flanks were secured by swamps, preventing the Americans from turning or easily getting in the rear of the British. On August 16, 1780, during the engagement at Camden, Gates's militia lines did indeed break. Gates had compounded his previous logistical and mental errors by placing the militia on his left side and trying to attack the British with them. In addition, the British army typically placed its most reliable units on the right side of the line. In this instance, the best British units were fighting the most unreliable Patriot units. Using conventional military tactics, Gates had the militia attempt to bore in on the British and fight them in the traditional style. Without proper training, or even bayonets, this attack soon ground to a halt. Cornwallis ordered an almost immediate counterattack, which virtually swept the field of the militia and opened the Continental troops to being hit in the front and flank with destructive musket fire.[19] Banastre Tarleton led a group of British horsemen and hit the Americans in the rear, causing the remainder of the American lines to rupture and disintegrate.

The ensuing disintegration of the American lines ended in a rout and utter defeat of epic proportion. In the end, Gates's army lost almost two thousand men at Camden, roughly one thousand killed and wounded and one thousand taken prisoner. British losses were a little more than three hundred killed and wounded. As the militia lines broke, General Gates was seen riding as fast as possible toward Charlotte, North Carolina, where he arrived on August 16, and Hillsboro, North Carolina, where he ended up on August 19. Alexander Hamilton, a colonel serving with George Washington at the time, stated:

Was there ever an instance of a general running away as Gates had done from his whole army? And was there ever so precipitous a flight? One hundred and eighty miles in three days and a half! It does admirable credit to the activity of a man at his time of life. But it disgraces the general and the soldier.[20]

The aftermath of the Battle of Camden was very discouraging to the Patriot cause. A few days after the battle, Tarleton, with the aid of Loyalists, surprised a band of South Carolina militia and a small number of regulars under Thomas Sumter in camp, dispersing and capturing many of the militia. With the dispersing of Sumter's force, Cornwallis's western or left flank was free from Patriot interference. According to historian John W. Gordon, "The Americans had no body of organized troops left in South Carolina. Those who still had the will to fight could only do so as guerillas."[21] Those guerillas would eventually wreak havoc on Cornwallis's army, though, and would plague him and has men throughout their unwelcome stay in the Carolinas.

Francis Marion would emerge as one of the most romantic figures of the Revolution. His exploits operating from the swamps and lowlands of South Carolina would not only bolster the Patriot cause and form the basis for numerous far-flung myths, but would also truly hinder the advance of Cornwallis's army and cause him great concern for the safety of his right flank. Operating from the lowland swamps that are now under modern-day Lake Marion, the aptly named "Swamp Fox" and his group of Patriot militia attacked, harassed, outran and defeated the British and Loyalist forces sent to suppress him. Marion was an extremely capable militia officer who understood one of the key maxims of partisan warfare: do not fight the way your enemy wants you to fight. Outnumbered as he almost always was, Marion used speed, surprise, audacity and maneuver to his advantage. His men would seemingly emerge from the mists or in the dead of night to attack an unsuspecting British or Loyalist force and retreat to safety before the superior weight of the main British force could be brought to bear. In fact, Marion would become so successful that Cornwallis would detach Major John Wemyss and a sizeable force to chase him to ground.

As successful as Marion was in his role as a partisan officer, the American militia system was a detriment to sustained military operations. Members of the Continental army enlisted for a period of years, and members of state regular infantry units did likewise, but militia were called out for a period of months or until a local emergency had dissipated. Often the militia would avail themselves of any excuse to quit the field and return home, or they would simply vanish and return home at their pleasure. On the surface, this may seem to be a scandalous thing, but there were underlying issues with the militia that regular Continental units did not have. For one, the regular units were usually made up of young, unmarried men who had little that tied them down to home. The militia, on the other hand, quite often were married, operated in local areas and had family and economic issues that compelled them to return home at seemingly inopportune times.[22] As a result, militia operations were not sustained enough to please the Continental officers, and the animosity between the militia leaders and the regular officers did not make for a smoothly functioning war effort at times.

The period following the defeat at Camden was the darkest for hope of American success in the war. It seemed that everywhere the British were on the march, their armies inexorably devoured territory each day. Cornwallis had adopted a very loose policy of dealing with his army at this time. If an organized fighting force is in contact with civilians very long, there will inevitably be instances that are unsavory, and Cornwallis's stay in South Carolina was no exception. The modern military has rules against fraternization with enemy civilians to protect against this very thing, but no such rules were in place in 1780. In addition to rape and pillaging, one particular issue was a wholesale attack against Presbyterian churches, which many Britons felt were little more than pits of sedition. There were many instances of churches being ransacked and some even set on fire in an attempt to cow the population into submission to the authority of the Crown.

Major James Wemyss of Cornwallis's command was one of the principle perpetrators of terror in the South Carolina hinterland. He was given the task of quelling the attacks of Patriot militia on the eastern or right flank of the British army and set about completing this task in a manner that would cause locals to flock to the colors of the Patriot militia. He had roughly four hundred men and authority from Cornwallis to confiscate horses, burn dwellings and hang those who had committed acts against the British. Wemyss paid special attention to the homes and property of the men who rode with Francis Marion in an attempt to bring the "Swamp Fox" to battle and destroy his partisan band once and for all. Marion was too smart to fall for an engagement and moved his force toward North Carolina and safety. Marion did furlough his men who lived nearby to go home and help protect their families. Unable to get at Marion, Wemyss contented himself with burning homes, shops, mills and even a Presbyterian church in the hamlet of Indian Town. The result was that Wemyss was hated only slightly less than Tarleton, and the population of that portion of South Carolina would support the militia and the partisans with renewed fervor as the war dragged on.[23]

In studying history, there is a commonly accepted phenomenon known as the law of unintended consequences. This law bore fruit with the persecution of the Presbyterians and would end up swelling the ranks of the Patriots. The

Scotts-Irish formed a majority of the population in the western backcountry of both Carolinas. This group of people was fiercely loyal to family and was sensitive to anything that could be perceived as a slight toward them. Initially, they had stayed out of the Revolution and had not actively participated in the militia or political gatherings beyond their own locales. The attack on the Presbyterian Church helped change their stance in regards to the Revolution since many of them were staunch members of the sect. As the British army and its associated units penetrated deeper into the Carolinas, the Scotts-Irish would play a crucial role in their ouster and subsequent defeat.

Governor Rutledge had successfully escaped Tarleton's Legion that summer and had made it to the safety of North Carolina, where he continued his efforts to fight for South Carolina, but the British had other ideas. South Carolina was officially reorganized, with a royal governor installed and a Loyalist militia set up to pacify the countryside. While the times were especially dark for the Patriots, the British were unable to maintain the tightknit control over the colony that they desired and anticipated. The hard hand of men such as Wemyss and Tarleton pushed many people into the Patriot fold, bolstered by the success of Patriot leaders such as Marion and other partisans who were operating in the state.

The militia of Patriot leaders such as Thomas Sumter and Francis Marion continued to wreak havoc among the Loyalists in the countryside as well. At this time, South Carolina was experiencing a war for the hearts and minds of the people. To quote Mao Tse-tung, "The conventional force loses if it doesn't win; the guerilla wins if he does not lose." This was especially true in the late summer and early fall of 1780 in the South Carolina backcountry. As in the north, the Loyalists were only able to control the areas where their forces were actually located. As soon as the Loyalist militia or British army moved on, the Patriots regained control and exacted their own revenge on those they suspected of collusion with the enemy or with whom they had an old score to settle.

In mid-September, Cornwallis began to march his army toward the crossroads town of Charlotte, North Carolina. Unlike the bustling, growing, banking center of today, Charlotte in 1780 was a sleepy hamlet of less than 500 people where two main roads crossed. The only force to oppose Cornwallis's army was about 150 Patriot militia commanded by Colonel William Davie. Even though outnumbered about 30 to 1, Davie put up a laudable defense of the town, inflicting far more damage than he took. Normally, Banastre Tarleton would have been in command of the Legion, but he was incapacitated with a serious fever. In his place was an officer of

The South Carolina Campaign

limited skill and uncertain leadership, Major George Hanger. In his attack on Davie's men in Charlotte, Hanger badly mismanaged the affair, and what should have been a simple brushing aside of a small militia band turned into a hot and bloody contest. In fact, it was General Cornwallis himself that had to order the Legion to attack, after two initial and startling repulses under Hanger, to dislodge Davie's men. Davie had previously stated that he would rely on the "firmness of the militia...to give his Lordship some earnest of what he was to expect in No Carolina."[24] This incident was a harbinger of what Cornwallis was to experience during his stay in Charlotte.

Colonel Davie combined forces with North Carolina militia general William Davidson. This combined militia force could not dislodge Cornwallis's army from Charlotte, but the men developed a plan to harass it almost nonstop. Mecklenburg County and the surrounding area would become known simply as the "Hornet's Nest" because of the Patriot activity. Couriers and foraging parties were especially attractive targets to the Patriots. Swarming upon these unsuspecting units, the Patriots would attack, take their spoils and retreat out of range of Cornwallis's main force. Cornwallis eventually had to employ his Legion dragoons and other mounted infantry to ensure that any communications got to the bases at Winnsboro, Ninety Six or Charleston. Using his elite forces in such a manner wore them down and reduced their combat effectiveness at a time when the campaign was just beginning to take a toll on the army as a whole. Even though the Patriot militia would come and go with startling irregularity, they were able to replace their losses and recruit more men while Cornwallis's army would continue to shrink. To compound this error, Cornwallis wanted to deal with the possibility of a threat to his left or western flank, from the western regions of North Carolina. The desire to solidify the flank would prove to be a disaster for his army and the Loyalist cause in the Carolinas.

Cornwallis sent Major Patrick Ferguson, his inspector of militia, along with a unit of Loyalists to either intimidate or suppress the Over Mountain Men. In August 1780, before the debacle at Camden, a group of Over Mountain militia had joined forces with other militia groups to harass British and Loyalist units operating in the Spartan District (near modern Spartanburg) of South Carolina. They had set up and successfully executed an ambush at Musgrove's Mill that left more than two hundred Loyalists dead, wounded or prisoners. This Patriot group even wanted to move into the interior of South Carolina and attack larger and more inviting targets, such as the British stronghold at Ninety Six. Word of the defeat at Camden changed their minds, and they began a precipitous withdrawal from the area.

Ferguson had been sent to pursue and eliminate this group of partisans at the time, but they had escaped into the wild country of western North Carolina, where the Over Mountain Men returned to their homes.[25] Unfortunately for Ferguson and Cornwallis, this would not be the last time that the Over Mountain men would be heard from.

Patrick Ferguson was born in 1744 in Edinburgh, Scotland, and at age fifteen he joined the army. During his service, he caught the eye of General William Howe, who would become a great benefactor of Ferguson. Ferguson showed himself to be a master organizer, trainer and rifle shot. At one point, Ferguson improved on a mechanism for a breech-loading rifle, now called the Ferguson Rifle, and even demonstrated it for the king.

When the British army sailed for America, Ferguson and his rifles went with it. Ferguson was given command of a special unit of soldiers armed with his breech-loading rifles and trained as elite light infantry. Unfortunately, Ferguson was wounded at the Battle of Brandywine and lost the use of his right arm, and his command was dissolved and reassigned. Ferguson trained himself to write and use a sword with his left hand as a consequence of his wounds. Even though physically disabled, Ferguson continued in the field, gathering intelligence about Washington's army. General Clinton became a fan of Ferguson's and took him on the invasion of South Carolina. At Charleston, Clinton placed Ferguson in charge of raising, organizing and training the Loyalist militia that would be used to pacify the state. General Clinton did not remain in South Carolina long after the fall of Charleston. Clinton's second in command, General Cornwallis, took over, and Ferguson was not part of his inner circle. Ferguson apparently took this to heart and was determined to win over Cornwallis through achieving victory.

Chapter 6

PRELUDE TO KINGS MOUNTAIN

Ferguson set off from Cornwallis's army with a group of about 1,100 Loyalist troops, many from the Carolinas, and a veteran group of Loyalist militia from New York and New Jersey. Their route took them to Gilbert Town (modern Rutherfordton, North Carolina), where Ferguson made a critical error in judgment. On September 7, Ferguson arrived in the frontier settlement and decided to use it as his base of operations. Soon Ferguson came into contact with the militia of Colonel Charles McDowell and, though accounts vary, routed them thoroughly and sent them scurrying back into the Watauga area for safety. However, while in Gilbert Town, Ferguson made himself and his little army quite a nuisance, confiscating cattle, breaking open homes and taking what they needed or wanted without regard. Ferguson's patrols, however, detected that they were not the only groups operating in the area and that large militia forces in the western and northwestern counties of North Carolina (some also in modern Tennessee) were waiting to enter the war.[26]

Ferguson had easily routed McDowell and his small band of Partisans, but given the information his patrols brought back, he became uneasy. While Patriot militia would not be able to keep the field for extended periods, they posed a great danger to his Loyalist force, especially in the isolated region around Gilbert Town. If the militia groups joined forces and attacked him, then he could very well face disaster, since he was out of supporting distance of Cornwallis's main force and would probably be greatly outnumbered. Ferguson seemingly had two options: he could stay where he was and face possible disaster, or he could move his army nearer Cornwallis's main force in Charlotte. Neither option appealed to the officer who many called "the Bulldog." Ferguson's military reputation was on the line, and disaster or retreat would place a stain on it that would not easily be erased.

Being a resourceful soldier, Ferguson devised a scheme that could possibly extricate him and his army from the predicament. With the war going poorly for the Patriots as a whole, and with the recent defeat of McDowell's men, Ferguson wanted to bluff the militia bands into staying put until he could leisurely return to the safety of Cornwallis's protection. In a glaring example of the application of the law of unintended consequences, Ferguson's scheme would have a decidedly deleterious effect and would arouse the anger of the people of the region.

On September 10, 1780, Ferguson paroled a young Patriot militiaman who had been captured by his army and set his plan in motion. The parolee was ordered to ride straight to Colonel Isaac Shelby in western North Carolina (now Tennessee), a respected leader of a Patriot militia unit, with a decree from Ferguson. The decree stated that if the Patriots did not desist from their opposition to British arms, he would "march over the mountains, hang their leaders, and lay the country waste with fire and sword." No written accounts of Shelby's reaction have been found, but the result of the decree is unmistakable. Shelby went from his home in Sapling Grove (modern Bristol, Tennessee) to Washington County (also in modern Tennessee), where he conferred with Colonel John Sevier on what to do. The men agreed that the best course of action was to "march with all the men we could raise, and attempt to surprise Ferguson by attacking him in his camp, or at any rate before he was unprepared."[27] Sevier attempted to borrow money to finance the pursuit but found that there was none available except what had been appropriated for the State of North Carolina. The tax collector, John Adair, stated that he had no authority to loan Sevier the money but reasoned that if Ferguson were driven off by its use, then he would be vindicated for loaning it. Between $12,000 and $13,000 were given to supply ammunition and supplies. Shelby and Sevier did not want to take all of the men in the area since Indian attacks were a constant threat, and the British had been trying to get them to attack the frontier. According to Shelby, "We had received information that they [Cherokee] were planning an attack upon us in the course of a few weeks."[28] Knowing that an Indian attack was coming, the fact that so many men still turned out to catch Ferguson shows the disdain of the people for the man and his recent actions. Shelby and Sevier also sent word to other Patriot leaders urging them to join the fight against Ferguson.

Prelude to Kings Mountain

The Patriot leaders set Sycamore Shoals in the Watauga area as the meeting place for the Over Mountain Men to gather. By September 25, 1780, a force of roughly eight hundred men, sufficient they thought to defeat Ferguson, had been gathered in the mountains, and they made their way south and east toward Quaker Meadows (modern Morganton, North Carolina). The group was joined at Sycamore Shoals by nearly four hundred militia from Virginia under Colonel William Campbell. Before they left, a local minister, Samuel Doak, pronounced his benediction on the men. The little sermon that he gave was about the trials of Gideon and his people, and Doak likened the Patriot cause to Gideon's. At the end, he offered up the following oath: "The sword of the Lord and Gideon!" The men replied "The sword of the Lord and Gideon!" and began their march.[29]

The people Ferguson was trying to intimidate were exactly the kind of people that such demonstrations of bravado failed to impress. The population of this area of North Carolina was predominately Scotts-Irish, who lived on the bleeding edge of what could loosely be described as civilization. They carved a living out of the forests, fought Indians, survived illness and lived their lives free from outside interference or outside help. They detested authority that was not of their own making or choosing and looked on all forms of government with a decidedly skeptical eye. Leaders such as Isaac Shelby, John Sevier, William Campbell and Charles McDowell were at the head of troops not through family contacts or wealth but through their actions as men in the communities. These were a people who thought little of talk and demanded action from their leadership.

To the people of the mountains and backcountry areas of North Carolina, Ferguson was little more than a blatant criminal. They had heard stories of Tarleton's and Wemyss's brutality, and they knew about the wanton disregard for lives and property that Ferguson had shown in Gilbert Town. The leaders of the Patriot militia decided that they must deal harshly with Major Patrick Ferguson by inflicting a severe defeat. The leaders sent word to Benjamin Cleveland, of Surry County, North Carolina, to join them in their pursuit of Patrick Ferguson. The various groups of militia began to rendezvous at Quaker Meadows at the end of September. The force that gathered was as follows:

Col. William Campbell with four hundred men from Washington County Virginia, Col. John Sevier with two hundred forty men from Washington County North Carolina [now Tennessee], *Col. Charles McDowell with one hundred forty men from Burke and Rutherford, who had fled before the*

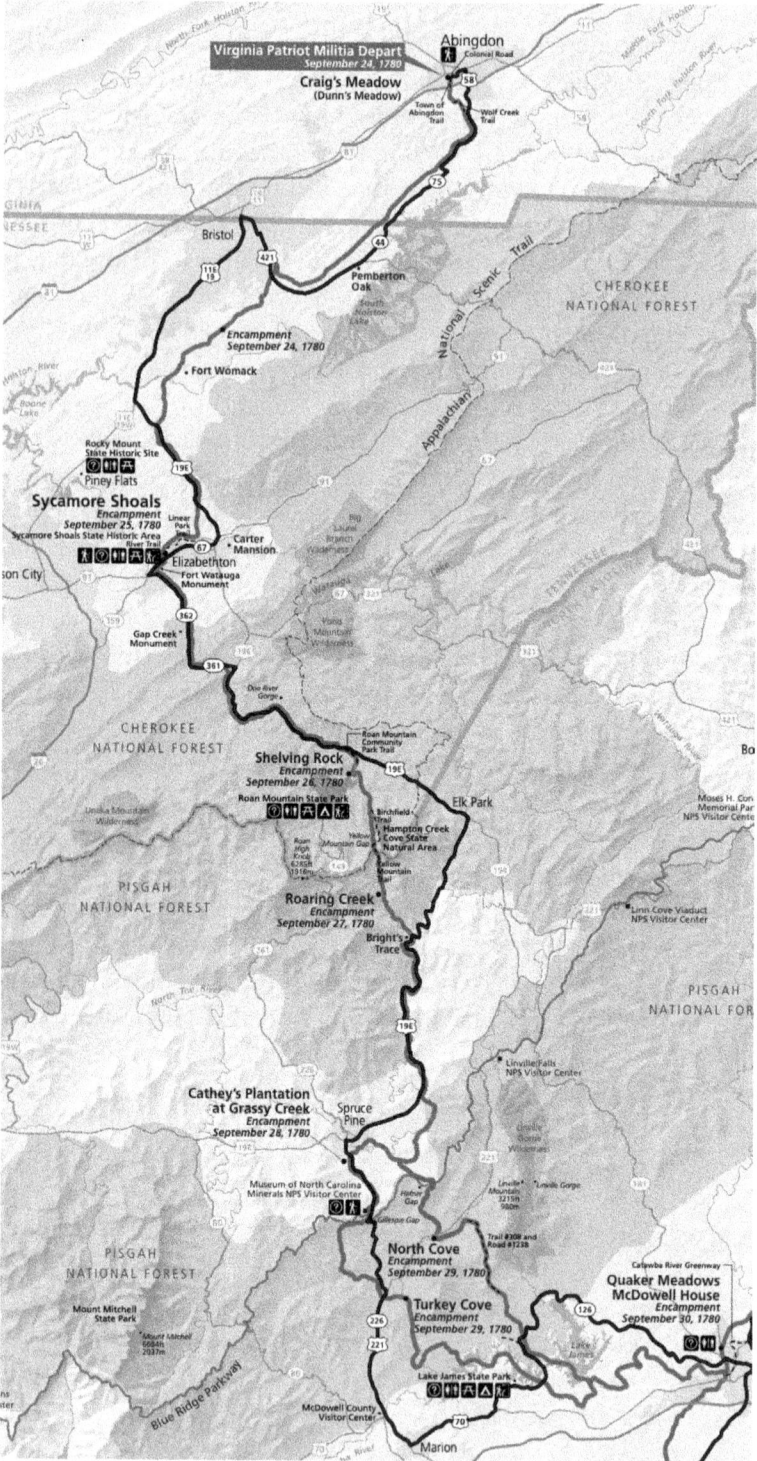

enemy to western waters, and two hundred and forty men from Sullivan county under my [Isaac Shelby] command...on the 30th we were joined by Col. Benjamin Cleveland with three hundred and fifty men from the counties of Wilkes and Surry, North Carolina.[30]

According to Shelby, just under 1,400 men marched from their homes on the frontier to catch Patrick Ferguson. They marched to suppress an enemy they saw as a threat to their very way of life and bring him to frontier justice.

Ferguson acted on the second part of his ruse at this time. He had planned a brief foray into upper South Carolina before he moved toward Charlotte. This was ostensibly to intimidate the South Carolina backcountry, as well as provide tacit evidence that he rejoined Cornwallis's army of his own free will. On September 27, 1780, Ferguson moved his force to try to intercept the remnants of Colonel Elijah Clarke's Georgia militia that had been fighting near Augusta and to overwhelm them.[31] As Ferguson moved south and east from Gilbert Town, Isaac Shelby and the Over Mountain Men were in pursuit, trying to catch him unaware. Ferguson moved to the Green River area, where he received some alarming news: the Over Mountain Men were approaching more rapidly than he had anticipated.

Ferguson is known to have sent word to Cornwallis at this time that he was en route, and many historians believe that he was silently asking the general for reinforcements. The couriers he sent were locals but were discovered, and they had to travel stealthily, and slowly, to avoid capture on their way to Cornwallis's camp. Unfortunately for Ferguson and his Loyalists, this message did not arrive in Charlotte until October 7, the day of the climactic battle. Ferguson also sent word to the commander at Fort Ninety Six in South Carolina to provide him with a large reinforcement of militia with which to help defeat Clarke. In light of what happened to him shortly thereafter, Ferguson's vision of destroying Clarke seems like sheer folly.

On October 1, 1780, Ferguson issued the following appeal to the Loyalists of the area:

Opposite and next four pages: Route the Over Mountain Men, Campbell's Virginia Militia and Cleveland's Surry County Militia took to Kings Mountain. *National Park Service.*

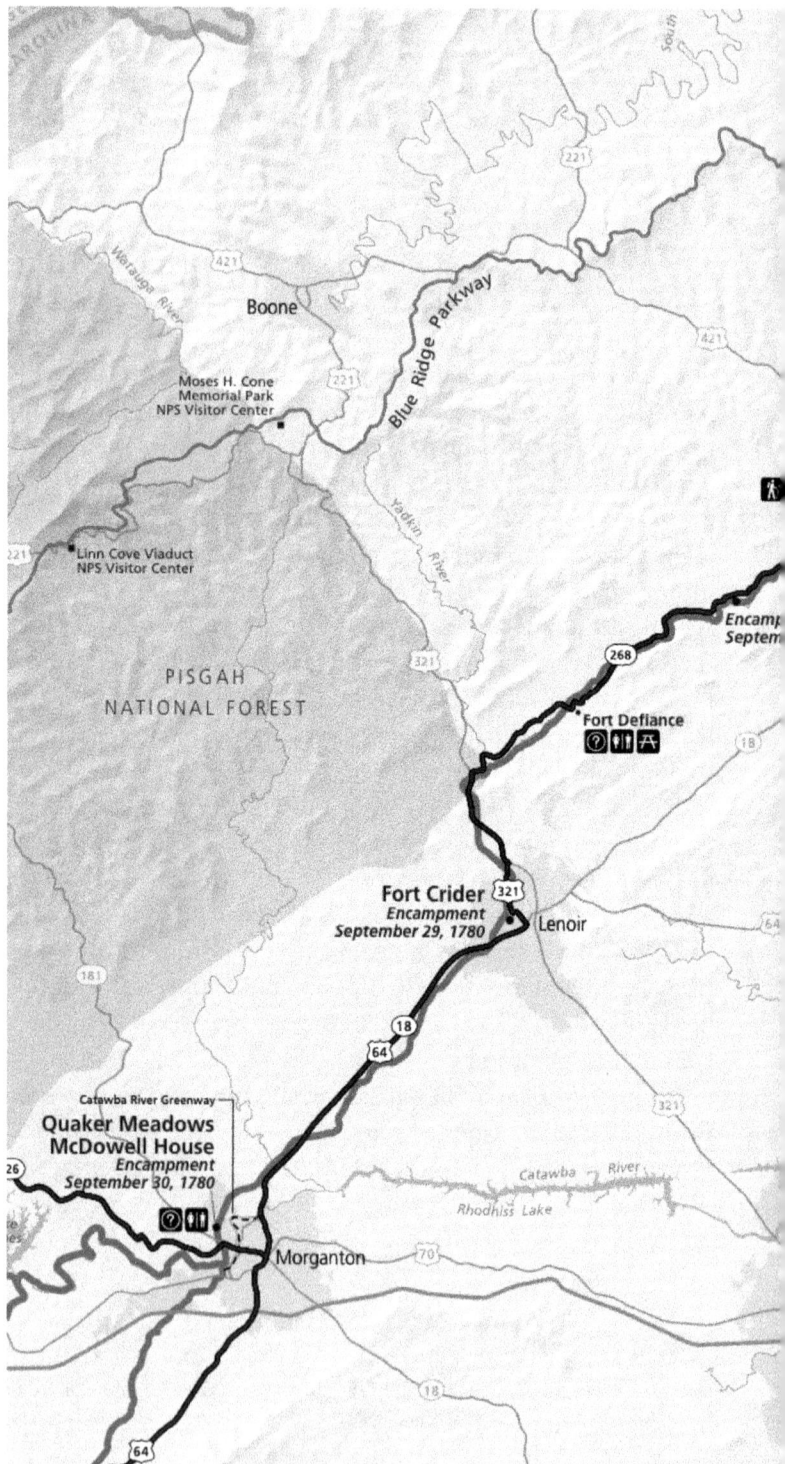

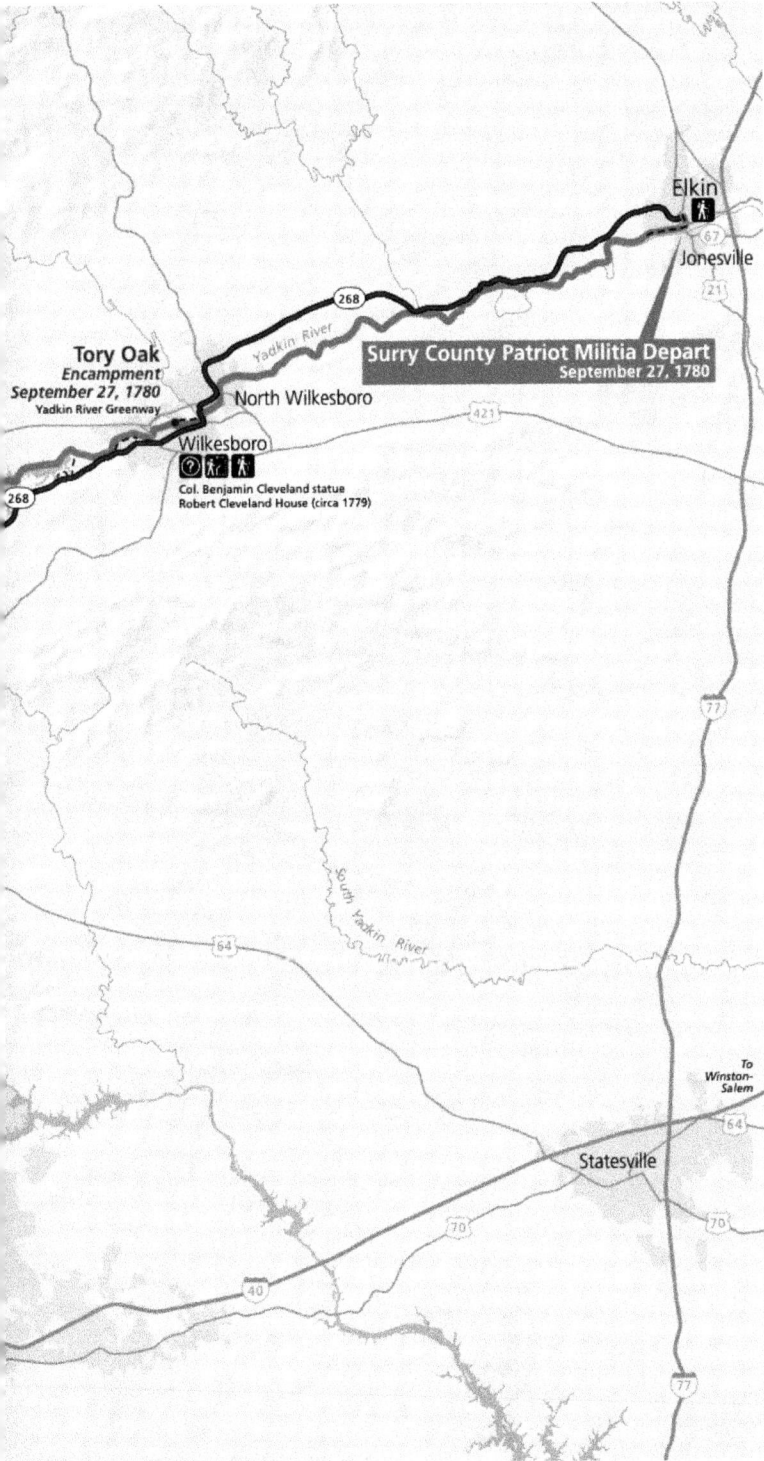

Elkin

67
Jonesville

21

268

Tory Oak
Encampment
September 27, 1780
Yadkin River Greenway

Yadkin River

Surry County Patriot Militia Depart
September 27, 1780

North Wilkesboro

421

Wilkesboro

268

Col. Benjamin Cleveland statue
Robert Cleveland House (circa 1779)

77

South Yadkin River

64

To
Winston-
Salem

64

Statesville

70

70

40

77

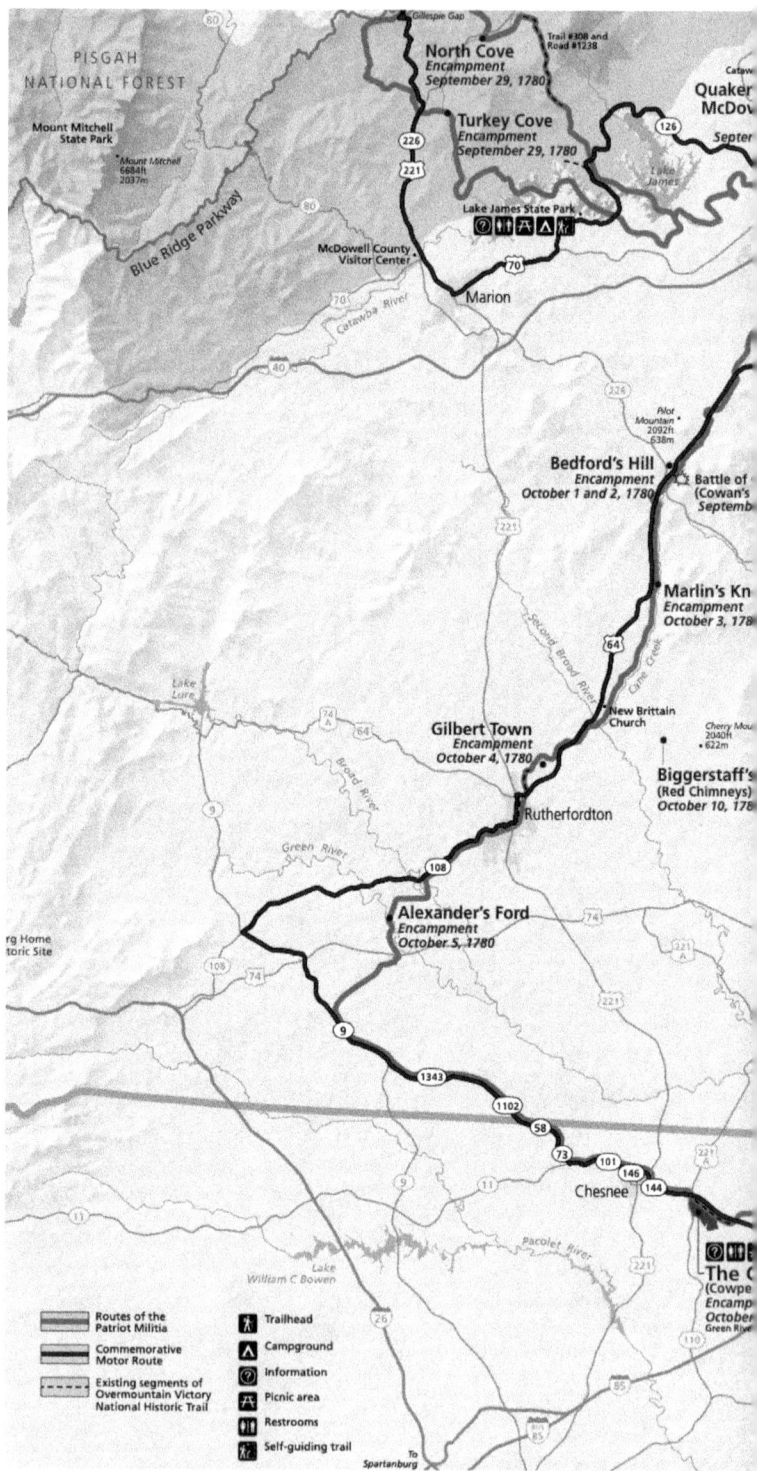

Gillespie Gap

Trail #308 and
Road #1238

PISGAH
NATIONAL FOREST

North Cove
Encampment
September 29, 1780

Catow

Quaker
McDo

Mount Mitchell
State Park

Mount Mitchell
6684h
2037m

226

Turkey Cove
Encampment
September 29, 1780

126

Septer

221

Lake
James

Blue Ridge Parkway

80

Lake James State Park

McDowell County
Visitor Center

70

Catawba River

70

Marion

40

326

Pilot
Mountain
2092h
638m

Bedford's Hill
Encampment
October 1 and 2, 1780

Battle of
(Cowan's
Septemb

221

Marlin's Kn
Encampment
October 3, 178

64

Lake
Lure

74

64

New Brittain
Church

Cherry Mou
2040h
622m

Gilbert Town
Encampment
October 4, 1780

Biggerstaff's
(Red Chimneys)
October 10, 178

Rutherfordton

9

Green River

108

Alexander's Ford
Encampment
October 5, 1780

74

rg Home
toric Site

108

74

221

9

1343

221

1102

58

73

101

221

146

144

Chesnee

William C Bowen

Pacolet River

221

The C
(Cowpe
Encamp
Octobe
Green River

110

85

Lake
William C Bowen

26

To
Spartanburg

85

	Routes of the Patriot Militia		Trailhead
	Commemorative Motor Route		Campground
	Existing segments of Overmountain Victory National Historic Trail		Information
			Picnic area
			Restrooms
			Self-guiding trail

Routes of the Patriot Militia

Battle of Kings Mountain
October 7, 1780

Gentlemen:—Unless you wish to be eat up by an inundation of barbarians, who have begun by murdering an unarmed son before an aged father, and afterwards lopped off his arms, and who by their shocking cruelties and irregularities, give the best proof of their cowardice and want of discipline; I say if you wish to be pinioned, robbed, and murdered, and see your wives and daughters, in four days, abused by the dregs of mankind—in short, if you wish or deserve to live, and bear the name of men, grasp your arms in a moment and run to camp.[32]

This call for reinforcements was made as Ferguson gained information that the Over Mountain Men were hot on his trail. In addition to the Over Mountain Men, Colonel Davie's dragoons that gave the Legion such a hot welcome in Charlotte were known to be on the march to help intercept him. All in all, Ferguson was at the center of a vast confluence of Patriot forces, and it was a place where Ferguson should have known not to be. Ferguson wanted to deal Clarke's men a decisive blow before he returned to Cornwallis, and this desire explains his slowness in moving from the area. The distance from where Ferguson was camped to Cornwallis in Charlotte was less than fifty-five miles, and a concerted effort would have placed him in the safety of Cornwallis's lines rather than on the ridges of Kings Mountain.

As it was, Ferguson moved north of the Broad River while moving slowly east. His route took him through the eastern portions of modern Rutherford County and through southern Cleveland County. By October 3, Ferguson's men had crossed Sandy Run Creek and then Buffalo Creek. They stopped at a large farm, known locally as Tate's Plantation, and there they set up camp for at least two days.[33] At Tate's Plantation, Ferguson sent another communiqué to Cornwallis stating that several Patriot militia units had effected a union and that he was on the road heading to Charlotte. He further stated that "three or four hundred good soldiers, part dragoons, would finish the business."[34]

Ferguson was being at the very least disingenuous in this letter to Cornwallis, as events will show that Ferguson was not on the march to Charlotte, but instead moving toward the ridges of Kings Mountain. Nineteenth-century historian Lyman Draper believed that Ferguson's final letter to Cornwallis demonstrated that Ferguson did desire to move directly to Charlotte and rejoin Cornwallis as soon as possible. Draper's main argument lies with the fact that Ferguson does not mention that he planned to make a stand on Kings Mountain, and if it was his intent to fight there, he would have likely said so. Ferguson and his designs are not that simple, though. He was in search of martial glory, and even though decidedly outnumbered and becoming outmaneuvered, a decisive battle fought within arms reach of the main army would redeem his reputation. Ferguson intentionally encamped on the high ground hoping that Loyalists and reinforcements would give him the opportunity to crush the Over Mountain Men, and he could rejoin the main army victorious. According to Loyalist Alexander Chesney, "We marched to King's Mountain and there encamped with a view of approaching Lord Cornwallis's army and receiving support; by Col Ferguson's orders I sent express for the Militia Officers [Loyalist militia] to join us here."[35] Even with Chesney's statements about Ferguson's desire to move toward Cornwallis, it doesn't explain Ferguson's inactivity and delay.

The Patriot militia pursuing Ferguson was not an army in a fundamental sense but rather a collection of units loosely termed regiments. This formidable band of riflemen did not have an overall commander, which could have served to help Ferguson and derail their attempts at defeating his men. At a council of war held while on the march, Colonel Isaac Shelby tried to establish a loose chain of command, yet his entreaties met without approval. The colonels did send word to General Gates in Hillsboro requesting to send them a commander, preferably Daniel Morgan, but a commander did not arrive before the battle took place. The Over Mountain Men would catch up with Ferguson and bring him to battle without any one person directing the engagement. This group of men, gathered from the fiercely self-reliant frontiersmen, would do battle with Major Ferguson in the same independent style in which they lived.

As Ferguson moved through what is now southeastern Cleveland County, his eye was undoubtedly drawn to the only prominence in the area, a series of hills and ridges known at the time as the Kings Mountain Range. Ferguson's army would end up on a low-slung ridge about one mile south of the North Carolina border. The ridge sat between seventy-five and one hundred feet above the surrounding area and was littered with old-growth trees—poplar, gum, oak and some pine—and bordered on the northern side from west to east by a small stream. Here Ferguson made his camp and probably awaited the arrival of Loyalist militia that had heard his call to arms, as well as the Legion reinforcements that Cornwallis may send. Draper quotes a letter from a Loyalist who was with Ferguson who said, "The situation of Kings Mountain was so pleasing that he concluded to take post there, stoutly affirming that he would be able to destroy or capture any force the Whigs could bring against him."[36] Ferguson apparently liked the defensive nature of the position and decided that he would make his stand at that spot. In fact, Ferguson has been quoted from his diary as saying the area on and about the ridge of Kings Mountain reminded him of the terrain near his boyhood home in Scotland. Ferguson is often quoted as saying to his men, "This is Kings Mountain and I am king of this mountain. God Almighty and all the rebels of hell cannot drive me from it!"

Many historians have asked why Ferguson would choose this spot to stand and fight when other defensible positions were very nearby. The answer lies in the terrain of the battlefield and Ferguson's imperfect analysis of its advantages and disadvantages. As discussed earlier, the high ground is the usual key to the battlefield, and the side that holds that high ground has a distinct advantage. On the ridge of Kings Mountain, Ferguson possessed the high ground but with one major error. There is a slight but very important difference between the military crest of a hill and the geographic crest. The geographic crest is the summit along the highest points, whereas the military crest is slightly lower and allows the placement of troops without their being silhouetted against the sky. Ferguson's 1,100-man force was on the almost bald, geographic crest of the ridge in the fall, when the leaves were beginning to fall from the trees. Almost 200 of his men had been sent on a foraging expedition in the area, leaving Ferguson with roughly 900 men to defend the ridge. The area around the ridge had ample trees from which to erect breastworks to fire from behind or to construct abatis—logs with a series of sharpened stakes or limbs sticking out front that forces attackers to slow down. Alexander Chesney had the following to say about Ferguson's position: "Kings Mountain from its height would have enabled us to oppose a superior force with advantage, had it not been covered with wood which sheltered the Americans and enabled them to fight in the favorite manner."[37] Chesney apparently failed to see the inherent strength and resources that the ridge and wooded slopes provided for a defensive force.

Even with his error in placing troops on the geographic crest, Ferguson still had the opportunity to create a formidable defensive position. Ferguson apparently did not take any such measures. There were no defensive works established on the ridge to provide cover for the defenders. There were no abatis erected to slow attackers. The lines of retreat were not identified nor protected in any manner. Ferguson parked his wagons near his headquarters, but no further efforts at improving his position have been discovered. Throughout the day on October 6, 1780, Ferguson's men rested, made a few patrols and awaited reinforcements. Ferguson was less than one day's march from Cornwallis, and his inaction proved fatal for himself and his Loyalist army.

Prelude to Kings Mountain

While Ferguson was ensconcing himself on Kings Mountain, the Over Mountain Men were hot on his trail. While camped in the Flint Hill area, the Over Mountain Men were joined by a group of militia from the South Fork area under Major William Chronicle.[38] These men were from the forks of the Catawba River in and around modern Lincoln County, North Carolina, and were referred to simply as the "South Fork Boys." The backcountry men had joined the Over Mountain Men in their quest to destroy Ferguson. The union of multiple militia forces would present Ferguson with an enemy potentially present in overwhelming strength. This combined group of militia was less than one day away from catching up with Ferguson.

The Patriots' immediate destination was the Cowpens, an area just northwest of modern Gaffney, South Carolina, where locals would herd their cattle to be sold or slaughtered. During this portion of the march, it has been legend that the Over Mountain Men began to lose their ardor in catching Ferguson. They had left their homes virtually undefended from the Cherokee, and there was considerable plunder to be had from Loyalists in the area close by where they now marched. As the leaders grew worrisome and restless, Colonel Edward Lacey, a militia leader from the backcountry of South Carolina, met the group and relayed precise information that Ferguson was nearby.[39] This meeting, and eventual union of forces, emboldened the Patriots, and they marched for the Cowpens en route to catch Ferguson at Kings Mountain.

October 5 was a bad day in the Patriot ranks, even though those ranks had recently swelled in number. Horses that had been ridden hard and been treated poorly were wearing out. Men who had tramped over the mountains, through the streams and across the foothills were now footsore and tired. The colonels picked about seven hundred of their best men to continue the chase and go to the Cowpens. According to Isaac Shelby, "To pursue him unremittingly, with as many of our troops as could be well armed and well mounted, leaving the weak horses and footmen to follow on as best they could."[40] Only the best horses and the fittest men were sent to run Ferguson to ground. In Darwinian terms, only the fittest, strongest and most capable could survive on the frontier or in the backcountry, and of this group only the most elite were to continue the pursuit. Those who were now on Ferguson's trail were the cream of the Patriot militia.

While marching toward Kings Mountain, the Over Mountain Men observed a large party of Loyalists. Numbering approximately six hundred men, this force was probably bound for Ferguson to join him on Kings Mountain.[41] At times, discretion is the better part of valor, and the Patriots decided to leave this Loyalist group alone, else they delay catching up with Ferguson. On the afternoon of October 6, 1780, the Over Mountain Men arrived at the Cowpens. Near sunset that evening, Colonels Lacey and William Hill arrived in camp with about four hundred South Carolina backcountry militia.[42] The evening was spent killing cattle, gathering corn and cooking meals for the march.

On the morning of October 7, 1780, a group of a little more than nine hundred hand-picked men left the Cowpens, in the rain, to catch Major Patrick Ferguson. As they moved eastward, they understood that Ferguson was in the general area but were unsure of his exact whereabouts. The men crossed the Broad River at Cherokee Ford about daybreak and moved in a northeasterly direction hoping to make contact with Ferguson's force. At one point, a few of the officers felt that a halt was warranted to rest the men and the horses. When this happened, Colonel Isaac Shelby, who was in command in fact if not in name, lambasted the delay, stating, "I will not stop until night if I follow Ferguson into Cornwallis' lines!"[43]

Along the way, the band gathered intelligence from the people of the countryside, Loyalist and Patriot alike. One of the Patriot scouts had ridden ahead of the main body and found a house occupied by two young Loyalist women. A great ruse ensued. He went to the home, pretending to be a Loyalist who was searching for Ferguson to join his army. The young ladies were fooled and told the scout exactly where Ferguson was. When the main Patriot body came upon the house, they made a great show of dragging the scout outside and threatening to hang him.[44] When out of sight, the scout and the other men had to have had a hearty laugh at the ladies' expense. The information that was gained proved fortuitous to the Patriot cause. The ladies indicated that Ferguson's army was at an old deer hunting camp nearby. As luck would have it, Major Chronicle and one of his lieutenants recognized this as one of their own hunting campsites and knew the exact route to take.[45] Chronicle's men had hunted these woods for years and gave detailed descriptions of the ground held by the enemy.[46]

On the final march, the colonels developed their plan of attack. The Patriots would circle the hill and attack in unison: "Our plan was to surround the mountain and attack the enemy on all sides."[47] The plan was simple, brutal and relatively safe. Once one unit made contact and began to fire, the other units would follow suit. This arrangement left little to chance, which can be the bane of an army on the battlefield. The Patriots would not attempt to flank the enemy, but they would come straight ahead into the teeth of Ferguson's position from all sides. The Patriots would be firing

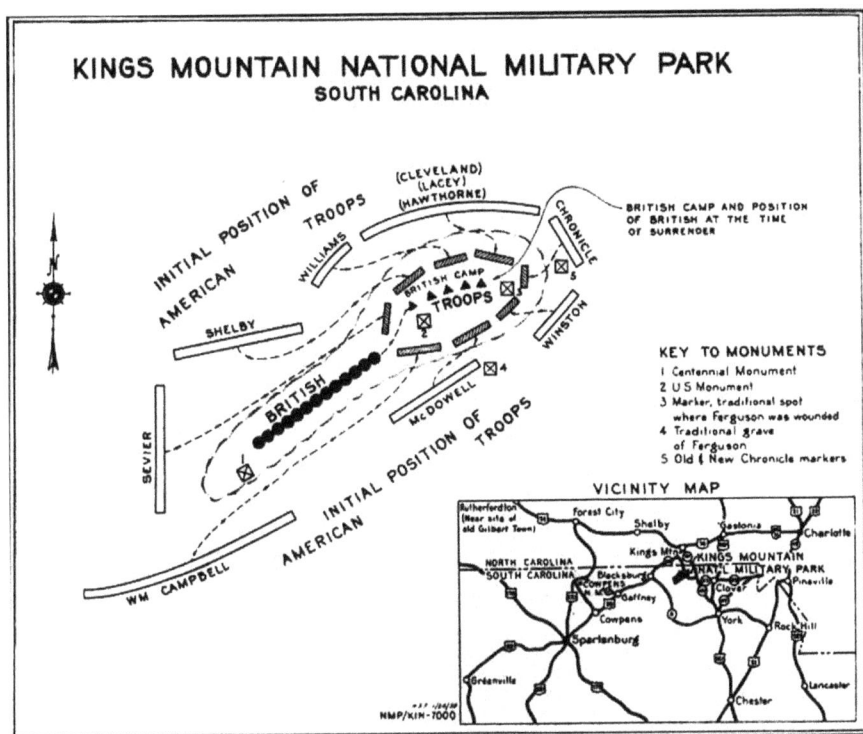

Map of Patriot and Loyalist positions at the beginning of the battle. *National Park Service.*

uphill, which would eliminate the possibility of friendly fire casualties until the crest of the hill was gained. Lastly, if the attack was repulsed, the lines of retreat were open in at least three directions, eastward toward Charlotte and Cornwallis being the one direction for which retreat would be unwise. All in all, it was a brilliant plan that offered the best chance of success with the minimum amount of risk.

Near what would become the battlefield, the Patriots captured several Loyalist pickets. Under questioning, they revealed Ferguson's position, exactly as the Loyalist young ladies had stated. One of the prisoners also revealed that Ferguson was wearing a red and white checked shirt. This information would make it easy for the Patriots to "mark him with your rifles," as Colonel Frederick Hambright urged his men in his heavily German-accented English.[48]

Chapter 7
THE BATTLE OF KINGS MOUNTAIN

On the morning of October 7, 1780, seventy-two-year-old local resident Arthur Patterson sent his sons to look for stray cows on their property near Kings Creek. Thomas and William Patterson were subsequently captured by the Loyalist militia and tied to trees near their camp to keep them from alerting any Patriot militia who might be lurking nearby.[49] Arthur became worried when his sons did not return by the noon meal, so he took his rifle and went to hunt for them. He ran into the Patriots moving into position for the attack. Patterson decided to join the Patriots in their assault on the ridge.

As part of the plan of attack, the Patriot force was split into two columns to surround the hill. One column, commanded by Shelby, would move to surround the ridge from the north, while the other column, commanded by Campbell, would do the same from the south. They would spread out along the base of the ridge until the order came to attack (an Indian yell peculiar to the Over Mountain Men).[50] In all, roughly 910 men would be in position to prove Ferguson's boast about being the king of the mountain wrong.

At 2:00 p.m., both columns prepared to move out and encircle the ridge. Colonel Cleveland took it upon himself to speak to the men of each unit, giving a rousing patriotic speech along with some sound advice.

My brave fellows, we have beat the Tories, and we can beat them again. They are all cowards…I will show you by example how to fight; I can undertake no more. Every man must consider himself an officer, and act from his own judgment.

Colonel Cleveland went on to exhort the men to retreat if need be but "not to run quite off" as the militia had been fond of doing on other battlefields. He also spoke to their manhood, stating that anyone who was afraid or feared that they would leave the fight should leave the group now. Many of the Patriots placed white cloth or slips of paper in their hats so that their comrades would be able to distinguish them from the enemy. Ferguson's Loyalist militia put sprigs of pine in their hats so that they could also be distinguished from the enemy in the smoke and din of battle. The Patriot officers ordered their men to recheck their weapons and apply a fresh prime to ensure ignition when the moment arrived. Many men also placed several lead shot in their mouths, to relieve thirst and to be ready for rapid loading in battle.[51] The horses were tied, and a few men left to watch them while most officers rode their horses into battle.

At about this time, Colonel William Graham went to Colonel William Campbell with word that he had gotten crucial information that his wife was ill at home and needed him by her side. This sort of nick-of-time information was highly suspicious to the leaders of the other Patriot units. Campbell asked Major Chronicle if Graham should be allowed to leave so near the battle. Chronicle, likely chiding Graham's seeming lack of fortitude for battle, said that "it's woman's business, let him go." Graham requested that someone ride with him as an escort, and the duty fell to young David Dickey, who protested but to no avail. Major Chronicle assumed command on this part of the field, even though he was junior to some other officers present, because of his intimate knowledge of the terrain.

Shelby sent out scouts to search for and silently dispatch any Loyalist pickets in the vicinity. To accomplish this, they carried the tools of frontier fighting: long, sharp knives and razor-edged tomahawks, tools with which they were familiar and skilled. As it turned out, the day was perfect for the Patriots to move undetected; the rain had softened the crisp autumn leaves, which would mask the sound of men and horses approaching.[52] The element of surprise was on the side of the Patriots for the time being.

Ferguson originally had 1,125 men in his camp on the ridge. This included the usual assortment of support personnel such as a drummer and doctors along with the soldiers. Ferguson also had two females in his company, Virginia Sal and Virginia Paul. These ladies apparently were cooks and laundresses for Ferguson—and also, more than likely, his mistresses. With more than one thousand men in camp on the narrow ridge, Ferguson would have had trouble physically placing any reinforcements that may come to him. This situation makes the decision of Ferguson to wait in the camp all the more perplexing.

Ferguson's force at Kings Mountain consisted of two main groups. One was the Provincial Rangers, also known as the Loyal American Volunteers. This group was recruited from New York and New Jersey and wore regulation British military uniforms, the infamous redcoat. Patriots recounting their battles with this unit at Kings Mountain are likely where the stories of redcoats in the battle comes from. This small unit, perhaps seventy-five men by the battle at Kings Mountain, would be Ferguson's shock troops during the fighting.[53] These men had fought Isaac Shelby and some Over Mountain militia one month earlier and were rightfully respectful of their fighting ability. The second group was the Loyalist militia, many from North and South Carolina. These men had been with Ferguson since the summer and were trained under him to fight in the British style. Ferguson's militia was armed with the usual Brown Bess musket but equipped with non-regulation bayonets. The bayonets that the Loyalists had were handmade and designed to fit into the muzzle of the musket. Sometimes books and other historical literature will refer to these weapons as "plug bayonets," which is an apt description. This group of men knew many of the Patriots they were fighting against, and there are many legends and accounts of combatants meeting one another face to face on the field of battle and afterward.

Even though the Patriots began the afternoon with surprise on their side, they did run into some problems. The first was that Major Joseph Winston's Surry County men, the ones sent to cut off Ferguson's line of retreat, went to the wrong hill. When they discovered their error, these men rode like mad through the forest to get in position for the attack. The second issue was the ground itself. The ridge drained water from the recent rain into a small stream that sat in the low-lying area on the northwest portion of the battlefield. This area turned into a swamp that probably bogged down the men of Shelby's column and caused them to be tardy to attack with the rest of the units.[54] The plan that the Patriots had devised was simple and direct, but even the best-laid plans can begin to unravel in close contact with the enemy and mother nature.

To compound matters, about 3:00 p.m. Shelby's men on the north side of the ridge were detected. Loyalists on guard duty spotted them moving in the trees and promptly opened fire. Their discharges ended Patriot hopes for a surprise attack and alerted the remainder of the Loyalists that something was going on.[55] The Loyalist officers had the drums beaten for the men to fall in, and Ferguson could be heard blaring his silver whistle that he used

Low-lying area and creek on the northern side of the battlefield that possibly delayed Colonel Shelby's men from getting into position for the attack.

to give orders. Ferguson was preparing his corps to battle the Patriots in the typical British style.

On the southwest slope of the ridge, one of Campbell's men had literally stumbled upon one of Ferguson's pickets. During the altercation, the Patriot soldier had to shoot the Loyalist to save himself. The ensuing noise alerted Ferguson and his officers that the Patriots were on at least two sides of the ridge and were likely preparing to attack. At this point, Campbell made an executive decision and decided to begin the attack. Even though all of the Patriot forces were not in position and the ridge was not surrounded yet, Campbell felt that an attack at this time stood a better chance of success than one when Ferguson had time to improve his defenses.

Campbell sent Captain Andrew Colville's mounted infantry up the slope to attack a fortified position. As the mounted men took off, Campbell admonished his remaining infantry to "Shout like hell and fight like demons!" As he finished his call, Indian war calls sounded all over and around the ridge.[56] The Loyalists knew that the Patriots were near, but these sounds had to unnerve many of the militia on top of the ridge. Captain DePeyster had heard the sound before in battling the Over Mountain Men in the Ninety Six district of South Carolina and called them "these damned yelling boys!" This would be an appellation that Shelby's men would wear proudly for the remainder of the war.

Ultimately, Colville's mounted attack was unsuccessful, and the survivors returned to the starting point. The men in Campbell's ranks saw the first casualties of the battle, and while saddened at the death of their friends, it brought their bloodlust to the boiling point. They moved up the hill and came to grips with the enemy. Colville's attack was the opening gambit in a battle that would last just over an hour. The premature start of the battle meant that not only was the ridge not completely surrounded, but also that the Patriot units were mixed up: "Much disorder took place in our ranks; the men of my column, of Campbell's column, and a great part of Sevier's, were mingled together in the confusion of battle."[57] McDowell had to move some of his men to the right to complete the encirclement called for in the plan. The Patriots had the ridge surrounded, though, and could now apply pressure from any and all points of the compass.

Southwest sector of the battlefield where Colonel Campbell's Virginians initiated the attack.

In the southwest sector of the ridge, Ferguson ordered a bayonet charge to dislodge Campbell's riflemen. As noted previously, close quarters combat is not the forte of the rifle, and Campbell's men retreated out of range. Campbell's Virginians suffered casualties in this bayonet charge, many inflicted with swords by Loyalist officers who charged on horseback.[58] Campbell's Virginians are conspicuous for a couple of reasons at Kings Mountain. One is that they had the farthest to travel of any of the Patriot groups to reach the field. Secondly, they suffered the largest losses of any particular unit on the field that day. And lastly, Campbell's men accounted for roughly one out of every three casualties suffered by the Patriot force. In addition, this group is known to have had at least five African Americans fighting with it, including four who were free.[59]

After the shock of the bayonet charge, the Patriot leaders rallied their shaken troops. They tried a second time to assail the hill and again were repulsed by a staggering bayonet charge. Campbell's men in the southwest sector of the battlefield attacked a third time and were yet again driven back by the bayonet. Captain DePeyster stated after the third attack and repulse that the Virginians were very nearly routed and that many ran away from the field.[60] According to Isaac Shelby, "The retreat was so rapid there was great danger of it becoming a rout."[61] The men were finally rallied, but it became increasingly difficult to do so. At this stage of the battle, the tide was against the Patriots, and it looked like Ferguson would make good on his boast of being king of the mountain.

Ferguson found himself in a quandary at this time. His men were able to easily brush back each successive Patriot attack, but they were not able to press their advantage. In order to shatter the Patriot lines and morale, the Loyalists needed to take the bayonet charge into the Patriot lines and beyond. If Ferguson did this, then he would create an opening in his lines on the ridge that would allow another group of Patriots to occupy and cut a portion of his men off. Continuing to beat off attack after attack, while successful, was using up the Loyalists' ammunition that could not easily be replaced. Ferguson was running out of time to secure a victory.

Colonel Isaac Shelby described the state of affairs on the north side of the ridge: "They repelled us three times with bayonet charges; but being determined to conquer or die, we came up a fourth time."[62] As the Patriots continued to assault the ridge, their unit cohesion was broken up. The men began to make their way up the hill by pairs and squads, something they had learned fighting Indians in the backcountry. As they worked their way up the slope, they used the terrain features and foliage to their advantage.

The Battle of Kings Mountain

The slope of the ridge as it faced Colonel Isaac Shelby's men. Note how men massed on the crest would be silhouetted against the afternoon sky.

Trees and rocks became protection, and a high or prominent tree became a sniper's nest. The Loyalists on the crest of the hill did not have one group to focus their volley fire on or to effectively charge.[63] The insect-like swarming effect of the small units ascending the hill effectively negated Ferguson's conventional tactics. Cornwallis may have called Mecklenburg County the "Hornet's Nest," but the ridge on Kings Mountain certainly earned that name as well.

Isaac Shelby was seemingly everywhere on his portion of the battlefield that day. His steady hand helped calm the men and urged them to greater exertions. Even with men such as Shelby at the helm, the action took a turn for the brutal. The small unit fights became hand-to-hand, and brutality ruled the day. Men fought with fists, knives, empty weapons, tomahawks and anything that they could find. One account of the battle states that Patriot captain William Edmondson became enraged after seeing so many of his family and friends killed. In one flurry of combat, he beat a Loyalist with his fist, grabbed him by the throat and dragged him down the hill from the summit.[64] Even though he was later mortally

69

The ridge facing Colonel Sevier's men. Note the way that the slope makes a sharp climb in this sector of the battlefield.

View of the Loyalist positions toward Colonel Isaac Shelby's men.

wounded and died, Edmondson's actions are indicative of the afternoon on the ridge at Kings Mountain.

The battle was initiated on the southwestern and northwestern slopes of the ridge, but the remainder of the Patriot force soon got into the battle. If you go to Kings Mountain National Military Park today and take the walking trail, one of the first markers you will come to is the William Chronicle marker. The original monument, which has been ravaged to illegibility by time and the elements, was one of the first monuments to Revolutionary soldiers. At this approximate spot on the eastern edge of the battlefield, Major Chronicle got his South Fork Boys into action.

The terrain on this part of the field is without a doubt the most rugged of the battlefield, and Chronicle's men had to traverse it to get to the enemy. The hill at this point is quite steep, with large rocks and logs littering the area. Charging up this slope under a hail of gunfire would be the ultimate exercise in military manhood. Chronicle got his men into formation, went to their head and exclaimed "Face the hill!" He had no more gotten the words out of his mouth than he was felled by a Loyalist bullet. Lieutenant Colonel Frederick Hambright assumed command of Chronicle's unit at this

Chronicle marker; the original marker erected in the early nineteenth century is on the left.

Terrain faced by Chronicle and Hambright's men on the eastern slope of the battlefield.

time. Hambright's men would attempt again and again to move up the hill over the next forty-five minutes. The South Fork Boys would continually work their way up the hill, and the Loyalists would charge with bayonets leveled, driving the Patriots away. As the Loyalists retreated back up the hill, the South Fork Boys would reload and begin to move up the slope again. While they never gained the summit of this portion of the ridge, they kept a number of Ferguson's men busy trying to dislodge them and prevented these same men from entering action on other parts of the field.

By the time Chronicle was killed, the vast majority of the Patriot force was engaging Ferguson's army with varying degrees of success. Ferguson's position on the crest of the hill was seemingly strong but was not having the success that such strength should have. The Patriots were attacking an elevated position manned by an enemy present in almost equal force and were having success. The reason for that lies in the terrain of the ridge and tactics employed by Ferguson. The ridge was covered with old-growth trees, as described previously, and these provided the Patriots with the ability to "give them Indian play," as the saying went, and move up and down the slope while under some shelter from fire. Alexander Chesney recalled that the Patriots "were able to advance in three divisions under separate leaders to the crest of the hill in perfect safety until they took post and opened an irregular but destructive fire from behind trees and cover."[65] Secondly, Ferguson trained his Loyalist militia to fight in the British style, and he clung to that style at Kings Mountain. Massing troops to charge an enemy is sound in the open field, but on a wooded ridgeline, fighting an enemy using irregular tactics, it is ineffective. Also, the tendency of soldiers posted on high ground is to fire high, and the shots go over the head of the intended target. One Loyalist militiaman, Drury Mathis stated that they "were very generally overshooting the Americans."[66] There are ample accounts of this taking place at Kings Mountain, thus the damage that theoretically could have been inflicted on the Patriots flew harmlessly over their heads.

As the fighting continued, the Patriots continued to have success and built on it. Patriot Leonard Hice, in his pension application, described his afternoon at Kings Mountain: "I shot 16 rounds...the way that I fought after my arm was broken was to rest my rifle against a tree and take sight."[67] Hice was wounded at least three times during the fighting. The Patriot movements

Terrain in Colonel Benjamin Cleveland's sector of the battlefield.

View from the Loyalist positions toward Colonel Cleveland's position. The natural advantage of this position should have been overwhelming.

and attacks frustrated Ferguson's ability to counter and bring force to bear. His men were acting bravely, charging and firing at the Patriots in waves, but their bravery was for naught. They were rapidly using up their ammunition, and the Patriots were continually drawing closer. This state of affairs is corroborated by Samuel Williams, a Loyalist combatant: "[A]nd numbers being without ammunition gave way, which naturally threw the rest of the militia into confusion."[68]

In fighting a textbook battle, Ferguson was playing into the hands of the Patriots. His superior fighting force was diminished by lack of a focal point for attack, his line of retreat was cut off, his men were expending ammunition that could not easily be replaced during the fighting and the fire of his men was having little effect compared to the expenditure. The successful Patriot tactics were not by design but rather through intuition and years of experience fighting Indians and Loyalists. They had intended to attack in unison, in a conventional military manner, but the initial failure of such movements by Campbell and others caused them to use the tactics that they knew. Their rifles were making deadly effect in the ranks of the Loyalists, especially those who were brave or unaware enough to expose themselves in the afternoon sun bathing the crest of the ridge. As the minutes passed, Ferguson's force was weakening, and the Patriot force was gaining the all-important momentum of battle.

During this time, one of Ferguson's mistresses, Virginia Paul, apparently thought better of her association with the "Bulldog" and ran from his camp. On her way down the slope, she procured a horse, supposedly released Thomas and William Patterson and galloped toward the Patriot lines. When she reached the nearest officer, she described Ferguson's dress, as well as where he was situated, and continued on her way. Paul was detained by the Patriots and eventually sent to Cornwallis's lines in Charlotte. Thomas and William took discarded weapons and joined the Patriots in their fight. Arthur Patterson, who fought with his newly freed sons against Ferguson that day, is listed as mortally wounded in the battle. He was not felled in the battle but rather lived until 1803, his will being witnessed by Frederick Hambright, son of Colonel Hambright.[69]

With the tide turned against them, the Loyalists began to take ever more casualties. The Patriots were experiencing a surge of momentum that carried them to the crest of the ridge. The summit was first gained in Shelby and Campbell's section of the battlefield, and at this point, the summit gently settles into a swale that runs the length of the ridge. As the Patriots gained this position, Loyalist accounts talk about the look of the men they were fighting. One Loyalist in particular said after being wounded that he lay still on the field else he be killed by Patriot fire. As the Patriots passed over him, he described them as appearing "like so many devils from the infernal regions." This same individual also stated that they "darted like enraged lions up the mountain." One can only imagine the looks on the faces and in the eyes of men caught up in the universe of battle against an enemy that was among the most hated of all. Remembering the battle, the same Loyalist soldier gave a physical description of the Patriot militia—that they were the most powerful-looking men he ever saw: "tall, raw-boned, and sinewy with long matted hair."[70] The appearance of such men on the crest of the ridge was not a sight that the Loyalists wanted to behold.

The battle had gotten out of hand for Ferguson. The end was near, and it would have been more prudent for him to attempt to fight his way out of the encirclement rather than to continue trying to parry Patriot attacks. Hambright's men never gained the summit on the eastern edge of the ridge and had been forced back with each bayonet charge, and it stands to reason that had Ferguson tried, at least a portion of his corps would have been able

Centennial marker. This marks the approximate location of where the Patriots first gained the crest of the ridge.

to escape. Ferguson's nickname, "the Bulldog," was fitting on the afternoon of October 7, 1780, though. Instead of fashioning a plan for escape or retreat, he placed himself at the head of his men, within rifle shot of the Patriots, and urged them on. He organized a last-ditch line of Loyalist militia and had them fire by volley and charge with the bayonet into the oncoming Patriots. The fire had a good effect, and the Patriots wavered.

More and more Patriots were gaining the crest of the ridge in seemingly overwhelming numbers. Ferguson's militia began to panic, and many men threw down their weapons and asked for quarter. At this point, the accounts of what happened on the top of the hill become confusing. There is evidence from a number of Loyalist sources that the Patriots fired into men trying to surrender. More and more Patriots were gaining the crest by ones and twos, and when they saw the mass of the enemy, many fired into them. At this point, even Ferguson understood that the end was at hand. He hastily organized a small force of men and tried to fight his way out of the encirclement and reach the safety of Cornwallis and the main army.

Ferguson was mounted on his horse, blasting his whistle and urging his small group onward. A number of Patriots saw the now infamous checked

The Battle of Kings Mountain

View along the top to the ridge at which Ferguson made his camp.

Marker that indicates where Ferguson may have fallen after being shot multiple times by Patriot rifles.

Traditional Scottish cairn believed to contain the remains of Ferguson and possibly one of his mistresses.

shirt and knew that their prey was at hand. These men of the backcountry and the mountains could hit a squirrel at one hundred yards, and a man-sized target was a simple matter at over twice that distance. Shots rang out, and Ferguson reeled in the saddle, dead from multiple rifle shots. A rifleman named Robert Young claimed that he had been the one to kill Ferguson with his weapon nicknamed "Sweet Lips." While Young might have been the one to hit Ferguson first, there were more than seven bullets that riddled his body within seconds. As he fell, one of Ferguson's feet became ensnarled in the stirrup, and his lifeless body was dragged around the crest of the ridge for a time until the Loyalist officers could get the animal under control.

In correspondence with General Cornwallis after the battle, Captain DePeyster gave the following account of the reasons for their defeat. "Their numbers allowed them to surround our post and ours was sufficient to form only a single line on top of the hill." A certain officer was killed, "which rendered the militia he commanded almost useless." And lastly the militia, "Tho the officers cut some of them down, they intermixed themselves with our detachment, and broke us in such a manner that we could no longer act."[71] One must conclude that Captain DePeyster is being at least somewhat disingenuous in his correspondence. For one, the Patriots only very slightly outnumbered the Loyalist force, and secondly, the Loyal American Volunteers were less than 10 percent of Ferguson's corps, the remainder being Loyalist militia that Ferguson has been training for months in the British style. The Patriot tactics, whether by design or not, and Patriot weapons had defeated the Loyalists, not phantom numbers or skittish Loyalist militia.

The Patriots had succeeded in crumbling the lines of the Loyalists. By penetrating Ferguson's position at one point, it invited the line to rupture in other locations. By the time Ferguson was killed, the entire Loyalist position was in real danger of collapse, having been pierced multiple times. With Ferguson dead and the corps in disarray, there was nothing left but to formally raise the white flag and save as many men as possible. This job fell to Ferguson's second in command, Captain Abraham DePeyster. According to Patriot ensign Robert Campbell, "Captain DePeyster raised the white flag and called for quarters; it was soon taken out of his hand by one of the mounted officers on horseback, and raised so high that it could be seen by our line."[72] Patriot soldier Private James Collins gives the following account: "[T]he enemy was completely hemmed in on all sides, and no chance of escaping—besides their leader had fallen. They soon threw down their arms and surrendered."[73]

The Battle of Kings Mountain

If the events surrounding initially gaining the summit are cloudy, those surrounding events after DePeyster's surrender are positively opaque. Isaac Shelby stated succinctly, "It was some time before a complete cessation of the firing, on our part, could be effected."[74] This statement whitewashes the issue in a way that makes it seem as if it were common on every battlefield in every war. In a way it was. In battle, passions are inflamed, men are trying their best to kill one another by all means necessary and in the case of a battle like Kings Mountain, in the blink of an eye out comes the white flag of surrender. The rules of warfare say that an army is supposed to treat those asking for quarter as prisoners who are not to be abused, but when the battle suddenly ends, it is incredibly difficult to turn off the adrenaline and aggression that have welled up during the contest. In the case of Kings Mountain, throw in the fact that Ferguson was an especially hated enemy and that his army was composed of Loyalists who were seen as traitors, and you have a recipe for atrocity.

DePeyster asked for quarter for his men, and many of the Patriots apparently refused to grant it. With the call for quarter from the Loyalists came an ominous response from many of the Patriots. There were cries of "Tarleton's quarter!" and shouts of "Give them Buford's Play!" If DePeyster and his command thought they were going to be able to simply throw down their weapons and be accorded safety, then they were sadly mistaken.

Two incidents provide us with some sense of what was happening on the crest of the ridge as the Loyalists tried to surrender. Joseph Sevier had been given a report, erroneous as it turned out, that his father had been killed in the battle. Young Sevier kept firing into the massed Loyalists until commanded to stop. He exclaimed tearfully, "The damned rascals have killed my father, and I'll keep loading and shooting until I kill every son of a bitch of them!"[75] In the other incident, Andrew Evins, who had fought with Captain Edmondson, and his comrades were seen firing into the Loyalists who had surrendered and had to be compelled by Colonel Campbell himself to stop the slaughter. About this time, Colonel William Graham, who had gone home to supposedly be with his ill wife, suddenly reappeared on the battlefield whooping and hollering in victory. One has to wonder what the officers and men in the Patriot ranks thought of his actions and subsequent display.

In later years, men such as Isaac Shelby would try to distance themselves from the events that happened after the Loyalists surrendered and would often speak of the events in generalities. This may be due to feelings of guilt or from simply forgetting the very sketchy details of that afternoon. Patriot soldier Charles Bowen showed a keen memory and no such need to gloss over his actions at the moment of surrender. In his pension application, Bowen had the following transcribed: "Declarant slipped behind a tree, cocked his gun, and shot the first man who hoisted the flag among the enemy and immediately turned his back to the tree, to reload."[76]

While Bowen filed this application many decades after the battle, its vividness is chilling. In his pension application, Joseph Hughes presents us with an interesting scene: "Gen. Williams of So. Carolina was Kill'd after the British raised their flag to surrender by a fire from some Tories. Col. Campbell ordered a fire upon the Tories & we killed near a hundred of them after the surrender of the militia & could hardly be restrained from killing the whole of them."[77] The anger of the Patriots is evident in this account, as is the possibility that all of the Loyalists were not fully committed to surrendering and felt like they needed to continue to fight. Loyalist officer Alexander Chesney sheds some light on the incident that Hughes related. After DePeyster sent out the flag of surrender, "The Americans resumed firing, afterwards ours renewed under the supposition that they would not give quarter."[78] With this in mind, it is easy to see how events could get out of hand on both sides. In *Kings Mountain and Its Heroes*, Lyman Draper presents two contemporary accounts that suggest that the Patriots did not, in fact, know what the white flag meant. If this were true, then it seemingly absolves the Patriots of their actions that afternoon, but even Draper himself admits that these accounts are probably exaggerations.

There were considerable feelings of ill will between the victors and the vanquished after the wanton killing had ended. As stated before, many men who fought at Kings Mountain knew one another and fought on opposite sides that afternoon. One bloody scene that has been written in many works on the Battle of Kings Mountain speaks of a set of brothers-in-law who fought on opposite sides in the battle. Near the end of the battle, the Loyalist, a man by the last name of Branson (or Brandon as is often stated), had been grievously wounded and saw his Patriot brother-in-law, Captain James Withrow, at the summit. He cried out for help, and on seeing him the Patriot said, "Look to your friends for help!"

With the battle over, it was time to assess the losses. The Loyalists had a geographically commanding position and roughly equal numbers, and it should stand to reason that the Patriots would suffer a greater number of casualties, but this was not so. Out of an estimated 910 men engaged, the Patriots lost 29 killed and 58 wounded, or less than 10 percent of their overall number. There are no accurate records of those who were captured,

The Battle of Kings Mountain

if indeed any were. The Loyalists lost 244 killed, 163 wounded and more than 670 captured out of 925 men engaged. In terms of killed and wounded, the Loyalists lost 44 percent of their total force, and when you factor in those who were taken prisoner, it reaches 100 percent of those who actually fought. The Battle of Kings Mountain was a most striking and significant defeat for the British and their Loyalist allies.

Chapter 8
AFTERMATH OF KINGS MOUNTAIN

As the night fell, the Patriots and their prisoners pitched camp together on the same field. The pitiable cries for water and help, especially from Loyalists, fell on deaf ears. Loyalist Alexander Chesney was taken prisoner by the Patriots and recalled that "[w]e passed the night on the spot where we surrendered amidst the dead and groans of the dying who had not surgical aid, or water to quench their thirst."[79] The men of the Patriot militia slept the kind of sleep that only a soldier during combat knows, while the Loyalist prisoners had to be fearful for their ultimate fate. Ferguson's body had been stripped naked, with the Patriots taking pieces of clothing and other articles for souvenirs and keepsakes. There were even reports that the Patriots had taken turns urinating on his corpse, though there have been no creditable eyewitness accounts.

The sun rose on Sunday, October 8, 1780, to a vast scene of suffering on the ridge. Men had lain all night in their agony from wounds and thirst. The groans and cries had become weaker and more pitiable. According to James Collins, "Next morning, which was Sunday, the scene became really distressing: the wives and children of the poor Tories came in, in great numbers. Their husbands, fathers, and brothers, lay dead in heaps, while others lay wounded or dying; a melancholy sight indeed!"[80]

There was great fear among the Patriots that Cornwallis would send Tarleton and the Legion to reinforce Ferguson. It was decided that the prisoners would be taken to the interior of North Carolina toward the Moravian towns (modern Winston-Salem) as soon as possible. The spoils of the battle were distributed—horses, swords, arms and tents—to the men and officers. James Collins again provides us with a description. "My father and myself drew two fine horses, two guns, and some articles of clothing, with a share of powder and lead."[81] The baggage that was not taken, along with the wagons, was summarily burned.

The bodies of the dead were hastily buried on the ridge. Patriot accounts indicate that there were very few proper graves and that the bodies were often covered with logs and rocks that could be scraped together. The animals of the forest eventually came to claim the flesh, with wolves, dogs and pigs being the main benefactors of the human slaughter. Local residents spoke often of dogs being mad, having feasted on the flesh of dead humans found on the battlefield. In fact, it was said that for many years that the locals were afraid to go out at night for fear of the wolves roaming the area.

By 10:00 a.m., the Patriots and their prisoners were on the march. The Loyalists not only were forced to march, but each man had to carry two muskets with the firing locks removed. Loyalist lieutenant Anthony Allaire's account, originally published in a letter written at Charles Town in January of 1781:

> *The morning after the action we were marched sixteen miles, previous to which orders were given by the Rebel Col. Campbell that should they be attacked on their march, they were to fire on, and destroy their prisoners. The party was kept marching two days without any kind of provisions.*[82]

Loyalist Alexander Chesney also provides a good description of the march:

> *Early next morning we marched at a rapid rate toward Gilbert's Town between double lines of mounted Americans; the officers in the rear obliged to carry two muskets each which was my fate although wounded and stripped of my shoes and silver buckles.*[83]

Chesney also describes the scant provisions: "Monday night when an ear of Indian corn was served to each."[84]

During the journey, many of the prisoners escaped or attempted to escape. These escape attempts enraged the Patriots, who shot or hacked to death many who they thought were trying to escape. One day during the march, a thunderstorm engulfed the column, and about one hundred prisoners escaped under the protection of its fury. The prisoners who could not keep up on the march were often trampled in the mire. In the evenings, the prisoners were thrown raw corn and raw pumpkins, just like pigs, much to the delight of the Patriot soldiers. The abuse became severe enough that Colonel Campbell issued the following order on October 11: "I must request officers of all ranks in the army to endeavor to restrain the disorderly manner of slaughtering and disturbing the prisoners."[85]

By October 13, the column and prisoners reached Bickerstaff's (or Biggerstaff's) plantation, which was northeast of Gilbert Town. The Patriots had been on the march for almost one week without rest and hounded by fears of Tarleton's Legion riding them down. Colonel Campbell at this time issued orders that if Tarleton arrived, they were "immediately to fire on Captain DePeyster and his officers, who were in front, and then a second volley on the men."[86]

In reality, Cornwallis did not put all of the pieces together about Ferguson's defeat until October 10. At that time, he sent Tarleton and the Legion out to support Ferguson and combine their forces to disperse the Over Mountain Men. What Tarleton found was information that Ferguson had been defeated, his army captured and Ferguson himself killed. Not only did he find out of the defeat and destruction of Ferguson's army, but also that the Loyalist cause in that area was a complete disaster as well. Tarleton's description of the defeat from his memoirs:

> *The destruction of Ferguson and his corps marked the period and the extent of the first expedition into North Carolina. Added to the depression and fear it communicated to the loyalists upon the borders, and to the southward, the effect of such an important event was sensibly felt by Earl Cornwallis at Charlotte town. The weakness of his army, the extent and poverty of North Carolina, the want of knowledge of his enemy's designs, and the total ruin of his militia, presented a gloomy prospect at the commencement of the campaign. A farther progress by the route which he had undertaken could not possibly remove, but would undoubtedly increase his difficulties; he therefore formed a sudden determination to quit Charlotte town, and pass the Catawba river. The army was ordered to move, and expresses were dispatched to recall Lieutenant-colonel, Tarleton.*[87]

Tarleton sums up the situation that faced Cornwallis after the battle at Kings Mountain nicely. The defeat did great damage to the Loyalist morale in the area, and without Loyalist militia there was no way that Cornwallis could pacify the countryside. If Cornwallis stayed in Charlotte, his army would inevitably grow weaker as men were killed and captured or deserted in this Hornet's Nest of partisan activity. North Carolina itself was a relatively poor colony and was not filled with provisions needed by the army. Cornwallis had to send foraging parties far and wide to support his men in what was at the time a tiny settlement, and this invited concerted attacks by Patriot militia. Cornwallis was also ignorant of what the Patriots were doing and what their plans were concerning his army of conquest. Ferguson and his force had been utterly destroyed, seemingly from nowhere, and Cornwallis was now in an exposed position. With the failure of the Loyalist militia to pacify the countryside, and now majority of this group no longer in existence, the left flank of the army was open to attack by Patriot militia.

In a strict military sense, Kings Mountain was devastating to Cornwallis's army. Cornwallis had two light units in his army that were able to move fast and strike quickly at the enemy. One of these was Tarleton's Legion, and the other was Ferguson's Loyalist militia force. The Battle of Kings Mountain took Ferguson's corps completely out of the military equation, leaving Cornwallis with only the Legion to fend off militia, suppress the countryside, gather intelligence about the enemy and protect columns on the march.[88] If a portion of his army met a similar fate in North Carolina, it could prove fatal to the king's cause in the South, thus Cornwallis was compelled to strategically redeploy his army into South Carolina.

On October 14, Cornwallis's army left Charlotte bound for the British strong point of Winnsboro, South Carolina. Positioning his army at Winnsboro placed it within supporting distance of Fort Ninety Six and Camden, both areas where Patriot militia groups were becoming active. From this area, he could winter his army and set up defenses against Patriot attack, as well as plan a possible second invasion of North Carolina. Cornwallis's first invasion of North Carolina had met a demoralizing end.

The end had not yet arrived for the prisoners of Kings Mountain, though. The day that Cornwallis marched out of Charlotte, a court-martial was held in the Patriot ranks to put some of the prisoners on trial. After the battle, a number of those captured were claimed to be "obnoxious" Loyalists who had committed murder, broken open houses and turned out women and children. While there may have been some prisoners who were guilty of such offenses, the real culprit was time, fatigue and old animosities. The Patriots had been on the march for almost one week, trying desperately to outpace Tarleton, who they thought was in pursuit. They were tired, ragged and hungry and had come to believe that the prisoners were intentionally slowing them down. The Patriots cultivated a hatred of the prisoners fueled by these issues.

Twelve field-grade officers made up the court-martial. The Patriots contended that the accused were allowed to call witnesses and that all arguments and evidence were carefully weighed in deciding the outcome. In the end, though, the Loyalists faced a classic kangaroo court where the deck was decidedly stacked against them, and the result was known before the trials began. Alexander Chesney in his journal called the proceedings a "mock trial."[89] In all, thirty men were condemned by the court-martial, these being described by the Patriots as the most obnoxious of the prisoners. Loyalist lieutenant Anthony Allaire, however, called those who were condemned "thirty of the most principal and respectable characters."[90] The evening of October 14 brought a grim scene to the backcountry of western North Carolina. A rude noose was fashioned and tied to a sturdy branch. The condemned were either set on horses and the horses walked out from under them, or they were stood upon logs and the logs were kicked away. Either way the execution was conducted, it was not enough to cleanly snap the necks of those who were hanged. As a result, the bodies twitched and struggled as the men slowly strangled, swinging in the gentle breeze. Three captains and six privates met their fate that evening, with all of the other prisoners forced to watch.[91] The senior Patriot leaders finally put a stop to the hangings and commuted the sentences handed down to the other twenty-one prisoners, but the great victory at Kings Mountain had been tarnished by the cruelty with which the Patriots treated their Loyalist captives.

The day after Cornwallis left Charlotte, the prisoners were marching toward the Moravian towns. The Patriots were an enterprising lot and decided to force the prisoners to pay for food and drink. Being on scant rations themselves, it seemed odd to the Patriots that they would furnish traitors with provisions at all, and if they had to, then it was a capital idea to turn a profit from the opportunity. Prisoners were forced to pay thirty-five continental dollars for an ear of corn and forty continental dollars for a drink of water. To make matters worse, the prisoners were not allowed to take so much as a drink while fording streams or rivers.[92] Several of the prisoners who were physically exhausted and unable to keep up were hacked with swords or run over by horses when they fell in the mud and muck of the roads. Eventually, the reduced party reached the safety of the Moravian towns, where life gained a semblance of normality, and then it was on to Hillsboro and the headquarters of the southern department. As the Patriots and their prisoners were nearing the Moravian towns, Alexander Chesney made a successful escape and would go on to fight the Patriots again on another Carolina battlefield.

The Patriot force that fought at Kings Mountain began to disband almost immediately after the battle. As in the tradition of the militia, now that the danger had passed, it was time to go back home and await for events to take their course. Some of the men who fought at Kings Mountain would return and face Tarleton and the Legion at Cowpens; others would live out their lives content with the satisfaction that they had defeated Ferguson and forced Cornwallis to change his base of operations.

Chapter 9
THE WINTER OF 1780–1781

After Cornwallis's exit from Charlotte, the town became a rallying point for the militia in North Carolina. Units from the backcountry and other areas moved toward the town that was formerly at the epicenter for Patriot resistance. Horatio Gates was still in command of the remnants of the southern army, which he also moved toward Charlotte to serve as a base of operations. The winter thus began with the two contending armies about fifty miles apart. Though the main armies did not mount major operations in the winter, the Patriot militia was active in harassing Cornwallis's forces whenever and wherever they could be found.

In late November, the Continental Congress recalled Horatio Gates because of his poor performance at Camden and subsequent aftermath. This time George Washington was given the charge of naming the general to command the southern army, and he appointed Nathanael Greene, a self-made military man who happened to be the right man in the right place at the right time. Greene had served with George Washington through the latter's trials and tribulations of the war. After serving as a successful line officer, Greene was appointed the quartermaster for Washington's army. He learned the ins and outs of supplying an army and scouring the countryside for supplies, as well as experienced the politics and infighting of the Congress. All of this would serve him well in his tenure as commander of the southern department.

While en route to Charlotte, Greene tried desperately to procure supplies for his new army. Stops in Philadelphia, Annapolis and Richmond met without success, and he was in low spirits upon arrival. In meeting with Governor Thomas Jefferson of Virginia, Greene lamented that Jefferson seemed more interested in talking about rights than protecting them. When he reached Charlotte and took official command of the army, he found out that it was a paper tiger. Official strength was 2,450 men, but only 1,632 were actually on hand, and of those less than 800 were fit for duty.[93] Greene is often quoted as saying that he could have done no better than Gates in the period after Camden, and the appalling conditions he found at Charlotte must have solidified that opinion. Greene sent men out to reconnoiter the rivers of northern North Carolina and southern Virginia, in particular the Yadkin and the Dan.[94] He felt that the ensuing campaign might take him in this direction, and he needed a firm understanding of the terrain and resources of the area.

George Washington had given Greene a daunting task; he was to build "an army to look the enemy in the face." In Charlotte, he found Daniel Morgan, now a brigadier general, in charge of a small force of militia. He found William Washington and Henry Lee with about two hundred cavalry. The remnants of the Maryland and Delaware regiments that were decimated at Camden were in place forming the core of the southern army. Much of the militia nearby was robust and had tasted success against Cornwallis at some point. All told, his force was very capable, but it was small and in some ways delicate. The colonels who commanded the militia units were very jealous of their authority, and the militia still came and went at their own choosing.

Greene set about trying to gain the support of the two most prominent militia leaders within his command, Francis Marion and Thomas Sumter. Greene would need these leaders and their men in his upcoming campaign, so their support was essential. A letter was dispatched to Francis Marion, in which Greene paid homage to him and the deeds his men had performed. Greene also asked that Marion provide him with intelligence on the enemy and the enemy's movements in his area.[95] Thomas Sumter was recovering from wounds he had suffered in the fall, so Greene went to see him in person. Sumter immediately urged Greene to attack Cornwallis's army. Sumter was a great combat leader, but according to historian John Buchanan, he was not a strategist and just didn't know it. The condition of Greene's army prohibited against any offensive action, but Greene promised to take the matter under consideration. Morgan and General William Smallwood agreed with Greene that any offensive action would be foolhardy at the present time.

Throughout the early winter, Greene continued to try and improve the supply situation of his army. He wrote to Governor Thomas Jefferson of

The Winter of 1780-1781

Virginia pleading for help in provisioning the Virginia troops who were in the army.[96] By the end of December, the army was expecting tents, shirts, shoes and other items that would be needed.[97] Greene wrote and begged for provisions from every quarter he could think of, but none was sufficient to provide his force with adequate food and forage. The area the army inhabited had been the center of the war for almost a year, and the local farms had been picked clean. The supply situation was acute, and without moving the army through the countryside and away from Charlotte, it didn't look to get any better.

Understanding that this small force could never directly stop Cornwallis's army from a second invasion of North Carolina, Greene developed a master plan. The key was to make sure the southern army did not endure a major defeat at the hands of Cornwallis; one more major defeat such as Camden could irreparably damage the Patriot cause in the South. With that in mind, Greene determined to use partisan tactics as much as necessary to weaken Cornwallis's army. Greene was reluctant to rely on militia due to their short enlistment terms and uncertain mettle in combat, but militia was the strength of his army and he had to play to their strengths. To achieve this end, Greene would violate one of the oldest maxims of warfare and divide his smaller force in the face of a superior enemy. One part would become a "flying army" that would lead Cornwallis, and Tarleton, on a journey through the backcountry, fighting small actions and bleeding the British as much as possible. The remainder of the army would position itself in the Pee Dee region and force Cornwallis to split his force to counter Greene's main army and the flying army. This split of the southern army would serve other purposes as well. The halves would be on the move, making it easier to forage and find supplies. Cornwallis would be obliged to follow both and would not be able to achieve a decisive knockout blow against either. According to Greene, "It makes the most of my inferior force for it compels my adversary to divide his."[98] As the halves moved in the countryside, Patriot militia groups would rally to them and expand their numbers. The entire plan depended on the halves being faster than the British in order to achieve success.

Daniel Morgan was selected as the leader of the flying army that included a potent mix of militia, light infantry and cavalry:

> *Sir—You are appointed to the command of a corps of Light Infantry, a detachment of Militia, and Lt. Col. Washington's Regiment of Light Dragoons. With these troops you will proceed to the West side of the*

Catawba river, where you will be joined by a body of Volunteer Militia under the command of Brig. Genl. Davidson of this State, and by the Militia lately under the command of Brig. Genl. Sumter.[99]

Greene's plan was for Morgan's flying army to operate in the rear and on the left flank of Cornwallis's army. He would be able to threaten the British stronghold of Ninety Six, as well as provide support to Greene's force if Cornwallis made a concerted effort to defeat it. Also, Morgan hopefully would be able to get the local militia to sally forth and join the cause in large numbers. Greene went on to give Morgan the following instructions: "The object of the detachment is to give protection to that part of the country and spirit up the people—to annoy the enemy in that quarter."[100]

Morgan was initially excited and accepted the command with enthusiasm. He believed that his command would number upward of three thousand men of all arms, which would be enough in his opinion to do a proper job.[101] Greene had given him about five hundred regulars, or Continentals, one hundred dragoons under Colonel William Washington, and the rest of his corps would be composed of militia under the aforementioned Davidson and Sumter among others. The expected level of militia support never materialized for Morgan and made his assignment all the more difficult.

On December 21, 1780, Morgan and his flying army set off from Charlotte, North Carolina, and headed southwest. Morgan had been given instructions from Greene to act "either offensively or defensively as your own prudence and discretion may direct."[102] Morgan marched for four long days and finally stopped on Christmas Day. His corps had to march through driving rains and cross rain-swollen rivers before they reached the fork between the Broad and Pacolet Rivers.[103] He made camp at Grindal Shoals on the north bank of the Pacolet, at the plantation of the local Loyalist leader Alexander Chesney, and began to develop his plans for annoying the British and spiriting the people. Morgan requested swords so he could mount a number of his best riflemen and create ad hoc dragoons and requested packsaddles so he would not be slowed by ponderous wagons carrying his supplies.[104] Morgan also requested that he be allowed to take his corps into Georgia to secure better provisions for his men. Greene turned this request down based on the distance he would be from the main army and the danger of being cut off if Cornwallis unexpectedly marched.

Thomas Sumter was one of the chief thorns in Morgan's side at this time. If fighting Cornwallis and his bloodhound Banastre Tarleton wasn't enough, Morgan had to deal with the bruised pride and ego of "the Gamecock." The

The Winter of 1780–1781

backcountry militia colonels were almost to a man jealous of their authority and guarded it carefully, and Sumter was no exception. When Greene sent Morgan into the area, Sumter felt that it was done without his knowledge and that Greene meant for him to take orders from Morgan. Sumter was enraged by this and ordered his commanders to ignore orders from Morgan and refuse to join his corps. In light of the setbacks Sumter had been dealt during the summer of 1780, it is logical that his pride would be stung, but his actions in the face of Cornwallis's army bordered on the absurd if not downright treasonous. Morgan sent Greene word of Sumter's orders on January 15, and Greene responded:

> *I am surprised that General Sumter would give such an order…but it is better to conciliate than agravate matters, where every thing depends upon voluntary principles, I wish you to take no notice of the matter, but endeavour to influence his conduct to give you all the aid in his power.*[105]

Greene at least seemed to understand the nature of the Carolina militia and the sensitivity of their leaders, even if it exasperated him. Morgan would get little help from Sumter, but Greene could not afford to alienate the popular leader completely if he was to defeat Cornwallis.

Morgan had yet another problem militia leader to deal with as well: Colonel Andrew Pickens of South Carolina. Pickens was not a native of South Carolina but had moved there from Pennsylvania in the mid-1760s and had married into the powerful Calhoun family. While not a notable orator, Pickens was the type of man who was a natural leader in the backcountry. He was relatively tall and slender according to most accounts and had proven his bravery time and again against the Indians, British and Loyalists. The Indians had in fact named him Skyagunsta, which means "Border Wizard Owl" and denotes one who was a great warrior, a name that fit Andrew Pickens.

When the British invaded Georgia in 1779, they set their sights on parts of South Carolina as well. The British and their Loyalist allies were especially keen to exact a measure of revenge against those whom they felt were Patriots or were considered too lukewarm to the cause of the king. In response to this British and Loyalist incursion, Pickens led a group of four hundred Patriot militiamen into battle at Kettle Creek on the Savannah River. His force overwhelmed and defeated a Loyalist and British force of almost twice its size. Pickens's militia had shown itself to be a force to be reckoned with in South Carolina.

With the fall of Charleston in 1780, the outlook was grim for Pickens and his men. Being one of the only viable military forces in South Carolina, they had to decide whether to continue the fight. His superior was General Andrew Williamson, who might have been the only Continental authority, military or civilian, left operating in the state, and he called his officers together to make a decision. The British had promised paroles to those who threw down their arms and took an oath not to fight against the Crown. After analyzing the situation, Williamson and his officers decided overwhelmingly to stack arms, accept paroles and go home. Pickens understood that his parole meant that as long as he did not fight against the British again, he and his men were in effect neutrals.[106] As long as Pickens was out of the war, there was very little hope that the men of his regiment would join Greene and Morgan. The British, however, would embark on a policy that would push the reluctant Pickens into Morgan's camp and into a very prominent role in the battle at Cowpens.

With Greene now in Charlotte, and Morgan's flying army operating in the area, Patriot militia leaders Thomas Sumter and Elijah Clarke practically begged Pickens to break his parole and join them. Pickens refused, saying that he was honor-bound by his parole not to take up arms. Clarke tried to entice Pickens and Pickens's men into joining them by passing his regiment near and through Pickens's plantation. Pickens was apparently perturbed by this incursion, as he still refused to join the Patriots or renounce his parole. The same could not be said for all of the men of his old regiment, though, and some did join the Patriots on their march to join Greene.

The British were fearful that Pickens would decide to break parole and join the Patriots. Pickens had been an effective military leader in actions leading up to his parole, and his men had generally heeded his command during the period of their parole. Clarke's incursion on Pickens's plantation was spotted by the British, who sent a mixed force of regulars and Loyalist militia to disperse Clarke's men. In the ensuing battle, Clarke was seriously wounded and had to return home. Most of Clarke's Georgia militia headed back to Georgia, but the Carolinians in his force continued their march toward Charlotte. Pickens's plantation was damaged by the British during their skirmish with Clarke, and this would end Pickens's neutrality.

Pickens believed that the damage to his plantation was intentional and violated the parole to which he had sworn. Now that the British had invalidated his parole, Pickens felt he was no longer honor-bound to remain neutral. He was now free to join his old regiment and ride to join Greene and Morgan. Pickens was eventually able to muster only seventy of his men, but his name alone was worth many times that number in a battle. The Border Wizard Owl was back in the war and would play a prominent role in the coming campaign.[107] Pickens and his small group would join Morgan at his camp at Grindal Shoals on December 26, and Clarke's remnants followed a short time later.

General Cornwallis had designs on a second invasion of North Carolina at this time. General Alexander Leslie had landed at Charleston with 1,500 men and was advancing to join Cornwallis's army. They had originally been scheduled to land in Virginia and march overland to join Cornwallis in North Carolina, but the Patriot victory at Kings Mountain changed those plans and they landed in Charleston. When General Leslie joined Cornwallis, the latter would have a force of 3,500 men in his field army and a sizeable force to leave on the frontier.[108] According to Banastre Tarleton in his memoirs, the sheer size advantage that Cornwallis had over Greene meant that he could invade North Carolina at his leisure and with an expectation of success. Cornwallis's plan was based on the belief that there were as many, if not more, Loyalist inhabitants in North Carolina as there were in South Carolina. Cornwallis would be able to deal with Greene's limited army in detail and possibly drive it "over the Roanoke" or destroy it.[109]

Greene, implementing his own plan to split the army and send Morgan's corps into Cornwallis's rear and left flank, forced the British to change their plans. When Morgan moved west of the Broad River, Cornwallis had to take action. The fortifications in the area, specifically the fort at Ninety Six, were designed to stand up to an assault, but the Loyalists of the area would be in disarray. Winning and securing the hearts and minds of the people was a key piece of the puzzle for both the Patriots and the British, and Morgan's force operating unchecked would have a poor effect on the Loyalists. Cornwallis therefore ordered Tarleton with his Legion and units of light infantry to force Morgan back across the Broad. Cornwallis's orders to Tarleton were that if Morgan were within his reach, he should be "pushed to the utmost."

On December 27, word reached Morgan at Grindal Shoals that a force of Loyalists from Georgia had advanced into the South Carolina backcountry. Keeping in mind his assignment to "spirit up the people," Morgan detached William Washington's dragoons and about two hundred mounted militia to deal the Loyalists a severe blow. Nothing lifted the spirit of the Patriots and their families and rallied men to the cause like a victory over the hated Loyalists. The action would become known as the Battle of Hammond's Store, and it would set events in motion that would culminate in the Battle of Cowpens.

During the battle, the Loyalist forces broke and ran; in fact, they broke so easily that the Patriots did not lose a single man. The Patriots rode into the fleeing enemy and hacked a number of them to death, just like their archenemy Tarleton would have done. Washington did not stop with scattering the Loyalist force, but rather continued on to Williams Plantation. At this location, the British had a stockade fort, known as Fort Williams, that stood on the communication line between Fort Ninety Six and Winnsboro, so it was of strategic importance for the British. As Washington and his men approached, the Loyalist militia manning the fort simply fled. Washington's force wisely returned to Morgan's camp, but their actions would set Cornwallis and his army into motion. Cornwallis wrote to his superior, General Clinton, about the state of affairs:

> But the constant incursions of Refugees, North Carolinians, and Back-Mountain men, and the perpetual risings in the different parts of the province; the in variable successes all these parties against our militia keep the whole country in a constant alarm.[110]

Chapter 10

PRELUDE TO COWPENS

mbarrassed by the setbacks at Hammond's Store and Fort Williams and ready to invade North Carolina again, Cornwallis and Tarleton devised a plan to deal with Morgan and his pesky force. If Cornwallis's whole army turned on Morgan, Greene would be able to attack and possibly overwhelm Charleston. If Cornwallis turned his whole army on Greene, Morgan would be on his flank and to his rear and might possibly retake Ninety Six and other western outposts.[111] Tarleton's Legion would run Morgan to ground on the west side of the Broad, while Cornwallis would march his main force up the east side, parallel with Tarleton, to act as an anvil to Tarleton's hammer.[112] Greene had forced Cornwallis to split his force and act according to Greene's design; Greene was in essence dictating the action to Cornwallis. In terms of the often-fuzzy principles of warfare, Greene had the initiative and was forcing a reaction from his adversary rather than having to react to a superior force.

Cornwallis agreed with Tarleton's plan for dealing with Morgan and reinforced him with 250 extra men and at least one more piece of artillery. These reinforcements gave Tarleton a strength of 1,100 men to chase Morgan and destroy his corps. Upon the arrival of reinforcements, Tarleton set out to the northwest to find Dan Morgan and his army. Tarleton was confident of his success in this endeavor, having a poor view of the fighting prowess of the Patriots. His head-on attacks had carried almost every field on which he had fought in America, and his experiences in the south only fueled his belief in himself. One of his subordinates pointed out that of the reinforcements that Cornwallis had sent him, 200 men of the Seventh Regiment of Foot were raw recruits that had not tasted a major battle.[113] This state of affairs apparently did not concern Tarleton, and they moved out in fine spirits.

On January 4, 1781, Morgan sent the following letter to Greene from his camp on the Pacolet:

> *I have received no acquisition of force since I wrote to you...My situation is far from being agreeable to my Wishes or Expectation. Forage and Provisions are not to be had. Here we cannot subsist so that we have but one alternative, either retreat or move into Georgia. A retreat will be attended with the most fatal consequences. The Spirit which now begins to pervade the people and call them into the Field will be destroyed.*[114]

While Tarleton was sure of his success in the coming campaign, Morgan was anything but. Morgan had requested permission to move into Georgia, but a movement that far afield would leave him and Greene out of supporting distance of each other. Greene had envisioned Morgan's force being a thorn in the side of Cornwallis and building up the fighting spirit of the militia and population, but a movement into Georgia would effectively put an end to that mission. Moving so far southward would also eliminate the psychological impact of Morgan's army being among the people and their enthusiasm would falter.

From Morgan's letter it is easy to see that he was apprehensive of Greene's plan as it was unfolding at the time. If Cornwallis and Tarleton bore down on him, then retreat would be his only option, and Morgan specifically mentions the effect of such a retreat in his letter. Morgan also had major supply difficulties while in camp. His force and the militia operating in the area had picked the countryside clean of provisions, and the prospect for gathering more was not promising. The second request for a foray into Georgia was vintage Morgan in its aggressiveness, but it was not part of Greene's strategic plan. A few days before the Battle of Cowpens, Greene responded to Morgan's January 4 letter.

> *It is my wish that you should hold your ground if possible, for I foresee the disagreeable consequences that will result from a retreat...Col. Tarleton is said to be on his way to pay you a visit. I doubt not but he will have a decent reception and a proper dismission.*[115]

Prelude to Cowpens

Tarleton's force was delayed in catching Morgan by rain-swollen creeks and rivers in his path that made his march extremely taxing on men and animals. Tarleton had dispatched men to ascertain the location and composition of Morgan's force. For all his bravado and self-confidence, Tarleton wanted to leave little to chance. His spies reported back that Morgan's force was growing daily, contrary to Morgan's letter to Greene, and this situation made Tarleton request that the Seventh Regiment of Foot be permanently assigned to him for this operation.[116] Tarleton hoped to drive Morgan from the west to the east side of the Broad River and possibly bring him to battle on the ridges of Kings Mountain. In a communiqué to Cornwallis describing his intentions, Tarleton stated:

> *When I advance, I must either destroy Morgan's corps, or push it before me over Broad river, towards Kings Mountain. The advance of the army* [Cornwallis's main force] *should commence (when your Lordship orders the corps to move) toward Kings Mountain.*[117]

The recent rains and swollen waterways greatly hampered Tarleton's force. He spent considerable time trying to find suitable fords that would allow them to cross the Tyger and Enoree. On January 14, Tarleton had crossed both rivers and received intelligence reports that Morgan guarded all of the useable fords on the Pacolet. With Cornwallis's army wallowing in the muddy red clay east of the Broad, it was important for Tarleton to force Morgan to attempt to cross the river. Tarleton would drive Morgan on and force him to retreat, and if he turned to fight, then Morgan would do so with the Broad River at his back and Cornwallis pressing from the east. It would seem that Tarleton had Morgan in a trap.

Cornwallis was having an even worse time negotiating the country than Tarleton. Reinforcements under Alexander Leslie were slogging through the swamps and lowlands of South Carolina. They were originally bound for Camden but had been redirected by Cornwallis to join his force. In order for Leslie to complete the junction of his men with Cornwallis, the latter was obliged to slow his march to a crawl. Tarleton was on the scent of Morgan, and his reinforced Legion outpaced Cornwallis by a great deal. The hammer and anvil of Tarleton and Cornwallis was not in position to be brought to bear in the manner both men had envisioned. One of the maxims of analyzing historical events is that it doesn't matter what we know in the twenty-first century, it matters what the people at the time knew and when they knew it.[118] Morgan and Tarleton did not know that Cornwallis had slowed to a crawl and was not in position to cut Morgan off on the east side of the Broad. The decisions that both men made were developed based on the scant information that they had at that time.

Morgan was caught in a conundrum in the worst sort of way. He knew that Tarleton and Cornwallis were moving to eliminate his force. His camp at Grindal Shoals was vulnerable to being entrapped by the coordinated movements of Cornwallis and Tarleton. The logical solution would be to abandon the position, retreat northwestward toward the upper Broad or Catawba Rivers and save his army to fight another day. To retreat would cool the spirit of the people to take the field and would abandon the local Patriots to the whims of the Loyalists. In fact, early Morgan biographer James Graham contends that a retreat would have been little less disastrous than a defeat.[119] Morgan also had an additional problem: the enlistments of many of his militia were running out. These men wanted to go home, and only a personal plea by Morgan caused them stay the course.[120] Additionally, the Broad and Pacolet Rivers were considered boundaries by many of the militia groups. If Morgan went south of the Pacolet, part of his force would leave and return home; if he went north of the Broad, another portion of his little corps would likewise leave. Morgan had no good options at this point but determined that it was best to move northward, where he could supply his men and search for an advantage to exploit.

On January 14 and 15, Morgan began the process of pulling his men out of the Grindal Shoals area and toward the Broad.[121] Tarleton was on the march toward him and was rapidly approaching. Morgan's maneuver had all the looks of a retreat in the face of the enemy, and the men did not like it and would come to resent the retrograde movement over the next two days. Morgan was actually forcing Tarleton into a losing situation, though. Morgan's men had picked the area clean of supplies, and now Tarleton's army would have to subsist in an area devoid of provision while pursuing an army.

In the meantime, Tarleton was on pace to reach Morgan before Morgan was ready to receive him. Morgan had left militia to guard the fords of the Pacolet and keep him informed of British movements. The rest of Morgan's army was camped at Thicketty Creek and unaware of Tarleton's approach. On the evening of January 15, Tarleton had made sure that the Patriot militia had seen his men go into camp without crossing the river so that Morgan would think he had stopped for the evening. However, after nightfall, Tarleton and his men found a ford that was unguarded and crossed at dawn on the sixteenth without the Patriots seeing them. Tarleton was only about six miles from Morgan's army, and Morgan's men were unaware of his approach.[122]

Morgan was immersed in the process of marshalling his forces for the battle he knew was coming. Hannah's Cowpens had been the rallying point for the backcountry and Over Mountain Men who defeated Ferguson at Kings Mountain, and it became the rallying point for militia now. As units approached Morgan's area of operations, they made for this location. Morgan sent others toward the Cowpens to secure supplies and guard the roads. Morgan's force was growing with each passing hour, becoming stronger and more dangerous, while Tarleton's men were exhausting themselves by countermarching through the night and subsisting on very short rations. Morgan found out quite suddenly, however, that Tarleton was only a short march from his corps, and he ordered the men to move out with the utmost haste. This would have been a startling and disappointing event for men who knew Morgan's reputation and wanted to fight the British. Many men were busy cooking breakfast and had to shove half-cooked cornbread into their mouths and begin to march. On the evening of the sixteenth Tarleton knew that his prey was near: "[T]he British light troops were directed to occupy their position, because it yielded a good post and afforded plenty of provisions, which they had left behind them, half cooked, in every part of their encampment."[123]

Morgan set a grueling pace for his men. It was cold and wet, and Morgan's sciatica had to have been incredibly painful in those conditions, but Morgan's corps was literally in a race for its life. Failure to outpace Tarleton would be far more disastrous than any retreat could possibly be. Morgan's destination was the Cowpens, the area where the militia groups were designated to meet. From the Cowpens he could cross the Broad at Island Ford, which was about five miles beyond, and hopefully into safety in North Carolina. The men marched on the Green River Road, a muddy track that had been churned by the constant march of men and animals. In the Patriot ranks, the men began to curse Morgan for his retreat and backbreaking pace he had set. According to Thomas Young, who was a young volunteer in Washington's cavalry, "We were very anxious for battle, and many a hearty curse had been vented against General Morgan during that day's march for retreating."[124]

The British spent the evening of January 16 enjoying the fruits of the former Patriot camp. But while the reinforced Legion was getting a bit of rest, the Loyalist militia was out and scouting the area for the location and disposition of Morgan's corps. According to Tarleton, "Patroles and spies were immediately dispatched to observe the Americans…Early in the night the patroles reported that General Morgan had struck into byways, tending toward Thickelle [Thicketty] Creek."[125] A Patriot militia colonel had straggled too far and was captured by Loyalist militia. This colonel provided Tarleton with information on Morgan's force and helped Tarleton decide to continue his pursuit of Morgan and attempt to forestall any more reinforcements reaching Morgan. Alexander Chesney had recently joined Tarleton's army and was one of the Loyalists sent out to ascertain Morgan's position. The only thing he found out was where the Patriots were not, that his crops at his plantation near the Pacolet had been taken or destroyed and that everything of value had been removed.[126]

Tarleton seemingly had Morgan where he wanted him: on the march and fleeing the Legion. The adjutant general of the Hessians in Cornwallis's army left the following description: "Believing that he had forced General Morgan to retreat and that his force was superior to the rebels', he went in search of him General Morgan on the 17th of January."[127] At 3:00 a.m., Tarleton ordered his men forward up the Green River Road in pursuit of Morgan. As fitting the weather and its effect on movement in the Carolinas backcountry, Tarleton reported that the creeks and ravines made his advance on the American position exceedingly slow.[128] Just before dawn, Tarleton ordered a troop of cavalry to the front to serve as an advance guard. While Tarleton's men trudged through the mud and muck, Morgan's men were at rest or getting ready for the next day.

Morgan arrived at the Cowpens ahead of his men on January 16. He rode over the ground with a local man, Captain David Tramell, and decided that he would make his stand at that spot. After his ride with Tramell, there are several sources that indicate that Morgan stated the following, or some permutation of it: "Here I will beat Benny Tarleton or I will lay my bones." During the afternoon and evening, new units arrived to reinforce Morgan. According to Lieutenant Colonel John Eager Howard of Maryland, "[P]arties were coming in most of the night, and calling on Morgan for ammunition… They were all in good spirits…and expressed the strongest desire to check his [Tarleton's] progress."[129] Though there has been no definitive account of the number of militia Morgan had present at Cowpens, most modern estimates claim upward of 1,200 to add to the Continentals and dragoons.

The question begs to be asked: why did Morgan choose the Cowpens to fight a potentially decisive battle with Tarleton? His original plan was seemingly to cross the Broad and continue on into western North Carolina and preserve his army. One of the keys to his decision had to be the Broad River itself. While fordable in its current state, the crossing would be slow,

Prelude to Cowpens

View of the battlefield that the dragoons on Tarleton's right would have had as they cleared the wood line.

and Tarleton's dragoons were near enough that a great disaster could ensue. Crossing the major rivers would also lead to the loss of a significant portion of his militia and hence his fighting power. Later in life, Morgan estimated he would have lost half of the militia if he had crossed the Broad. The mountains, which could be seen from the field, were at least forty miles away, and Tarleton was pursuing too fast for Morgan to reach them. Fighting at the Cowpens allowed Morgan to get his army farther away from the danger of Cornwallis's main army, gather reinforcements marching to him and fight on ground of his own choosing.[130]

The actual field Morgan chose was a relatively wide and open plain dotted with a few trees. It had some gentle undulations and terrain features that would have a great impact on the battle, though. The field itself was used to herd cattle before taking them to market and was of limited size. Where the British would first be seen was a sparse wood line on the southern edge of the Cowpens. Here the field was approximately 220 yards wide, small enough to ensure a compact body of men and easy visibility yet wide enough for Tarleton to array his light infantry in traditional line of battle. As the British would move into their anticipated attack toward the Patriots, the field widened marginally to about 300 yards in total width.[131] This extra width would end up being crucial to the outcome of the battle. The field was bordered by a low-lying swampy area to the east and by a ravine and creek in the west. The field also contained two points of high ground that Morgan would use to his advantage. Looking at the field from the British perspective, there was a slope rising to a relatively low crest, a swale behind that crest and another slope up to a final low hill that commanded the field.

All in all, this relatively compact and open field was perfect for a European-style battle using the combined arms of cavalry and infantry at which Tarleton excelled. Many historians have been very negative toward Morgan's choice of this site for the climactic battle even though it ended in a major victory. Years after the war, Morgan offered the following explanation for choosing an open field to accept battle:

> *I would not have had a swamp in the view of my militia on any consideration; they would have made for it, and nothing could have detained them from it. As to covering my wings, I knew my adversary, and was perfectly sure I should have nothing but downright fighting.*[132]

While Morgan's explanation has been derided by modern historians, there are other reasons that Morgan chose the ground that may have some basis in his above statement. One reason is the swampy ground (though not a true swamp) that was not conducive to cavalry operations. If Tarleton planned to get in the rear of Morgan's men, he would have to ride far off and around the battlefield, and as Richard Winn told Morgan, that was simply not the way that Tarleton fought.[133] An additional reason was that the gathering militia groups were using the Cowpens as a rallying point. Men were coming from far and wide, and the Cowpens was a known local landmark that could easily be found. A final reason lies in the nature of the ground itself. The gentle rises and depressions, along with the confined nature of the field, would give Morgan a great advantage in placing his men for a defense in-depth. Terrain is the key to the battlefield, and in the Cowpens Morgan had the exact type of terrain that he desired for this battle.

Chapter 11

DOUBLE ENVELOPMENT
AT COWPENS

Morgan simply knew that Tarleton would attempt a powerful head-on charge with his infantry, their bayonets leveled and flashing, and would follow up with his dragoons. This was the Tarleton model that had been so successful in the South, and "Bloody Ban" wasn't the type to change what had been successful. Tarleton would be looking to destroy and rout the Patriots before they could finish their retreat, seemingly to the Broad. Tarleton's tactics were usually about as subtle as a thunderstorm, but they had proven to be extremely effective in other battles throughout South Carolina.

If Morgan can be taken at face value, then he had planned to turn on Tarleton all along. He meant to string Tarleton throughout the Carolina backcountry, chasing the flying army ever deeper into the area and ever farther from Cornwallis. Once Tarleton's army was worn out and footsore, Morgan would then look for an advantage and fight a pitched battle in a location of his choosing. In his after action report to Nathanael Greene, Morgan states:

> *My situation at Cowpens enabled me to improve any advantage that I might gain and to provide better for my security should I be unfortunate. These reasons induced me to take this post, not withstanding that it had the appearance of a retreat.*[134]

This statement seemingly makes it clear that Morgan had planned to turn and fight, but no matter the intentions and thought process that went into his decision, Daniel Morgan made Banastre Tarleton pay a steep price for pursuing his flying army through the South Carolina backcountry.

Given his belief about Tarleton attacking with his infantry in a head-on charge, Morgan's chief goal would be to devise a plan that could neutralize or absorb the initial assault and allow his men to fight in a manner that better suited their unique style. Morgan would utilize the respective strengths of each type of unit in his corps to its advantage and attempt to minimize its weaknesses. Morgan's army had a core of Continentals in whom he had total confidence, these remnants of the Maryland and Delaware Line would form the rock-solid base of the main battle line. To the flanks of these Continentals he would add the Virginia militia, former Continentals whose enlistments had expired and were fighting now as militia. The Virginians could be counted on to behave like regulars, and Morgan based his placement of this unit with that belief. The Continentals and the Virginians would be formed on and about the crest of the second hill in Tarleton's front. Behind this main battle line William Washington would wait with his dragoons. They would be out of sight of Tarleton and would be used once the battle reached the main line or if there was a point of danger during the battle. Morgan augmented this cavalry force with forty-five mounted volunteer militia. On the crest of the first hill in Tarleton's front would be the militia. They would be about 150 yards in front of the main battle line and would be expected to put up a prescribed amount of resistance. About 100 yards in front of the militia line would be a group of hand-picked riflemen who would act as skirmishers. Their job was to harass Tarleton into attacking, kill as many officers and men as possible and send him to spring the rest of the trap.

While Gates had tried to use the militia-like Continentals at Camden, Morgan had no such intention at the Cowpens. As we have seen before, rifles cannot stand up to bayonets, and trying to do so would be an exercise in futility. With this in mind, Morgan devised a ruse: the skirmishers would goad Tarleton into a rash attack and would pick off as many officers as possible before being compelled to retreat to the militia line. The militia would fire three aimed shots (or two shots, depending on the account) and then would retreat around behind the Continentals. Tarleton would think he had a great victory in the making and would run headlong into the Continentals on the main line. Since the militia withdrawal was planned, the Continentals would not become demoralized by it and would put up very stiff resistance. While Tarleton's infantry was trading volleys with the Continentals, the militia would reform and hit him in the flanks, and Washington's dragoons would follow up from their concealed position and sweep the field of Tarleton's cavalry. At least this seems to have been Morgan's plan on January 16, though the element dealing with the reforming of the militia is shrouded in uncertainty to this day.

The decision to offer Tarleton battle had been made, and a plan to deal him a crippling blow had been developed. After dark on January 16, Morgan held a primitive council of war and explained his plan to the commanders. It stands to reason that Morgan asked for input from veteran militia officers such as McDowell and Pickens as to their thoughts on how to defeat Tarleton. The plan, as put into place on January 17, was undoubtedly affected by what these veterans had to say. While the men in the ranks may have been happy about the decision to turn and fight, undoubtedly many of the officers, including the militia leaders, were apprehensive about the prospect. As the commanders left the council, their men were encamped just on the northern edge of what would become the Cowpens Battlefield. Morgan's corps had time to rest before the battle, unlike Tarleton's army, which was slugging through the mud and mire, physically exhausting themselves before a shot could be fired.

That evening, Morgan proved that he was a true leader of men and understood those who served under him. Thomas Young stated in his memoirs, "It was upon this occasion I was more perfectly convinced of General Morgan's qualifications to command militia than I had ever before been."[135] Morgan stayed up most of the night walking among the men, encouraging them, helping them and reassuring them. Young goes on to state that Morgan told the men that he would crack his whip over Tarleton as sure as he lived. As he went to the campfire of each company of militia, Young states that Morgan told the men: "Just hold up your heads boys, give them three fires and you will be free. Then when you return home how the old folks will bless you and the girls will kiss you, for your gallant conduct."[136] This was the exact type of encouragement that the militia needed in this grave hour. Each officer was ordered that his men have twenty-four rounds of ammunition to begin the battle. This would ensure a sufficient supply for the engagement and would let Morgan know how much each unit had on hand at any particular time, based on the fighting that the unit had done. Before he stopped for the night, Morgan issued the sign and countersign for the evening: "fire" and "sword."[137] Fire and sword—two words that had to have emboldened the spirit of the militia, especially McDowell's men, who had defeated Ferguson at Kings Mountain. Morgan claimed that he then climbed a tree and prayed as hard as a man could. With the stakes at hand, it makes sense that Morgan would beseech the almighty to help him in the cause.

In preparation for the coming engagement, Morgan's baggage and supply wagons were sent north to cross the Broad. Messengers were sent out northward to hasten in reinforcements that were known to be on the move toward the Cowpens. Patrols were assigned to search for Tarleton lest Morgan be surprised by "Bloody Ban." Morgan had laid his plan, and nothing was left but to wait on the enemy to arrive. Tarleton's men had been on the road since 3:00 a.m., grinding toward the Cowpens. Just before daybreak, one of the patrols Morgan had sent out the previous evening spotted Tarleton's force and went galloping to report. The Patriot patrol had been spotted, but it was of no consequence; Morgan now knew that the battle was about to begin.

Morgan ordered his men up and to their posts. He went from camp to camp chiding the men with the phrase "Boys, get up, Benny's coming." This wake-up call had to send a chill through men who knew about the massacre of Buford or heard other tales of Tarleton's "quarter." The morning was cold, and the men were in the ranks when the sun began to rise over Thicketty Mountain to the east. Morgan sent small groups of horsemen to ascertain the position of Tarleton and determine how fast he was moving and from which direction he was coming.

Just as he had the previous evening, Morgan went among the men to rally their spirits. He stopped on the front line and bantered with the militia there. He rhetorically asked the men who would be the best shots that day, the militia of North Carolina or the militia of Georgia. These men in the skirmish line were crack shots, and if their compatriots witnessed them missing a redcoat, they would bear the ridicule for many months to come. Morgan had shrewdly turned the killing of British infantry and dragoons into a competitive sport. Morgan went to other militia units and gave classic eighteenth-century pre-battle speeches. He appealed to the mens' honor, their manhood and even their sense of revenge. It was recorded that when Morgan spoke to Pickens's militia, he was pounding his fist in his hand and making large sweeping gestures as he spoke. Morgan finished up by going to the Continentals, a group that had been severely treated by Tarleton and the Legion at Camden. He asked them to remember battles where they had been defeated and treated roughly and told them that they had to play their part this day in defense of liberty by exacting their revenge on Tarleton. The men took this in stride and cheered for Morgan, and according to most accounts, the men were in a fine mood. Morgan rode back to the second hill facing Tarleton, now commonly referred to as "Morgan Hill," and waited on

Double Envelopment at Cowpens

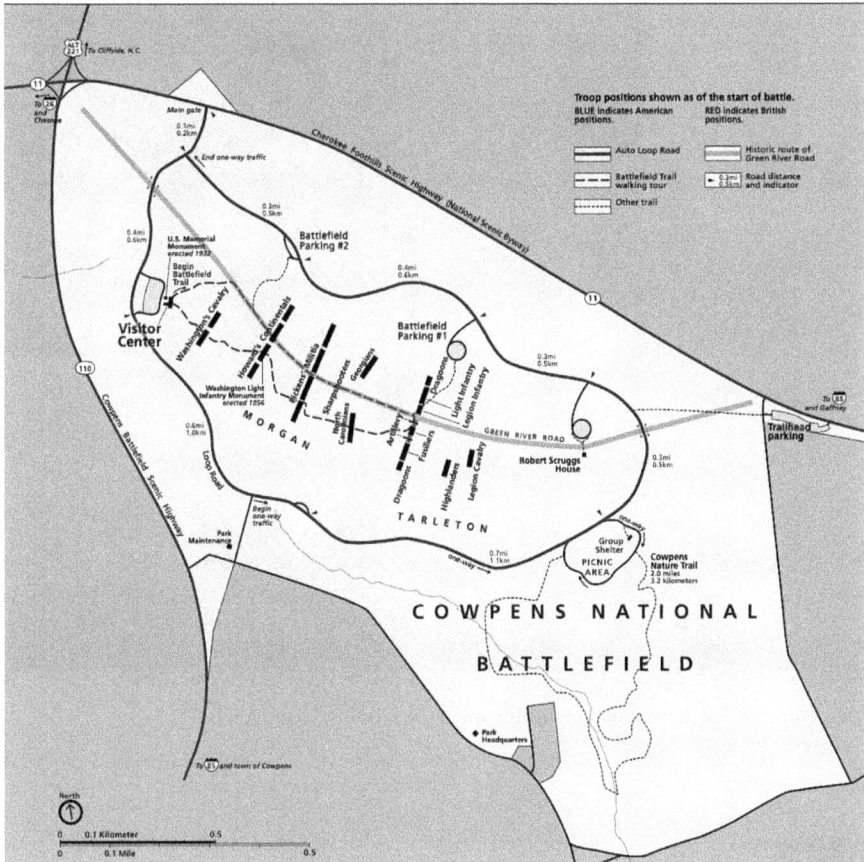

Map of the Cowpens battlefield including troop locations. *National Park Service.*

his horse for the battle to commence. Thomas Young tells us that the morning was "bitterly cold…and the men were slapping their hands together to keep warm."[138] The stress and strain of battle was about to warm the men more than any campfire ever could.

Tarleton's men emerged from the wood line shortly after dawn on January 17: the dreaded green-coated dragoons followed by the red-coated light infantry. James Collins stated, "About sunrise…the enemy came in full view. The sight, to me at least, seemed somewhat overwhelming."[139] As presumed, Tarleton was spoiling for a fight, and Morgan had set the stage to oblige him. The skirmishers were in position and took a number of pot shots at the dragoons as they came into view. Bullets whizzed by, and Tarleton made his decision to attack.

View from the Patriot militia line facing north toward the Continentals.

View of the field that the units on Tarleton's right would have had when they came out of the tree line.

Double Envelopment at Cowpens

The skirmishers had accomplished their first mission: they had goaded Tarleton into rash action. Tarleton sent fifty of his dragoons to drive in the pesky militia skirmishers. Tarleton also placed his two small cannons roughly in the center of his line and ordered them to fire at the Americans. Their fire had little effect, however, and they played no decisive role in the battle, even though Morgan had no artillery on the field. As the dragoons moved within rifle range, they began to take stunning casualties. Fifteen of the fifty horsemen who Tarleton had sent forward were casualties in just a few minutes. Some early accounts of this action state that the skirmishers followed orders and retired after the incident with the dragoons; this seems unlikely based on the events that followed, though.[140] Incensed, Tarleton dressed his ranks and formed a battle line for the requisite bayonet charge. Thomas Young stated, "It was the most beautiful line I ever saw."[141] Tarleton posted the Seventh Regiment (infantry) in his center, the Legion infantry and Light infantry on his right and the First Battalion of the Seventy-first Highlanders (infantry) on his left rear en echelon as a quasi reserve. Units of dragoons were placed to cover both flanks. Tarleton had no reserve or support to his rear except for the Highlanders and a few dragoons.[142]

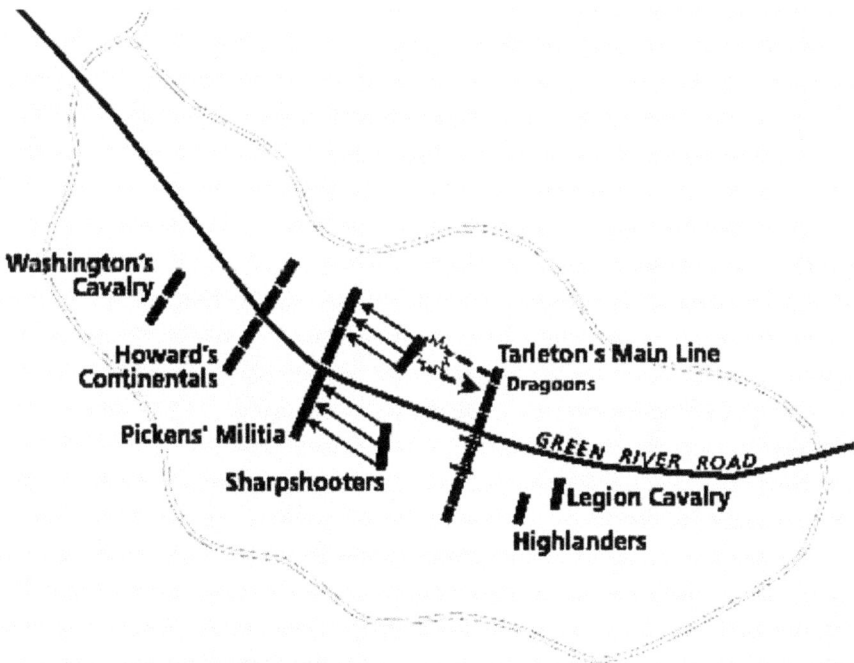

Map of troop locations and initial movements against General Morgan's skirmish line. *National Park Service.*

Morgan's plan had begun in fine form. His skirmishers had picked off a number of the dragoons, and Tarleton was preparing his typical attack. As Tarleton's infantry stepped off, everything but weapons and ammunition discarded, the skirmishers began to exact casualties from Tarleton's infantry. Officers shouting orders and giving commands were favorite targets of the skirmish line. A number of the raw British infantry from the Seventh Regiment fired at the skirmishers, without orders, and had to be stopped by their officers. As the bayonet-wielding infantry came closer, the skirmishers withdrew to the militia line or in some cases behind Howard's Continentals. McDowell's North Carolina militia conducted an almost textbook fighting withdrawal back to the main militia line, firing each step of the way. Tarleton witnessed the skirmishers withdraw and sensed that he had the battle well in hand. One massive charge against the militia and the day would be his. Now that the first line of skirmishers had fled, Tarleton was sure that the Continentals would be forced to retire if the militia was forced to flee as well. Tarleton's infantry moved forward, shouting and cheering the halloo, and Morgan's militia had to brace for the impact.[143] Tarleton wanted to get his infantry among the skirmishers quickly so they could use the bayonet to scatter them rather than being subjected to accurate long-range rifle fire for any length of time.

Morgan was with the militia at this point and told the men to respond to the British halloo with an Indian war whoop. "They give us the British halloo boys, give them the Indian halloo by G——."[144] Savage war cries went up along the line. One can only imagine that if Abraham DePeyster had been at the Cowpens that his blood would have run cold. It wasn't Shelby and his "damned yelling boys," but it was in fact many of their comrades in arms. The militia officers had to work hard to restrain their men from firing too soon. Thomas Young, who was on the militia line, relates, "Every officer was crying, 'Don't fire!' for it was a hard matter to keep us from it."[145] The men were ordered to let the British get in "killing distance" before they opened fire. This meant that the militia let the British get within seventy-five yards, very close if you have a rifle, before they opened up. At that range, there would be very few if any missed shots from the militia, which would savage the British formation.

The militia kept up a galling fire on the British infantry as they came on. The militia had a special affinity for the "epaulet men," or officers, and their orders were to single them out for their well-aimed rifle shots. The British attempted to return the militia fire but were ineffective as judged by casualty figures.[146] The British apparently fired too high, as years after the

Double Envelopment at Cowpens

View that the Patriots on the Green River Road in the skirmish line facing Tarleton's infantry would have had.

View that Tarleton's infantry would have had of the skirmish line to their left.

View of the Patriot militia toward Tarleton's oncoming Legion and the retreating skirmish line.

Another view from the Patriot militia line toward the skirmish line and Tarleton's attacking infantry.

battle people walking the field found bullets embedded in trees as high as thirty feet. According to Thomas Young, "The militia fired first. It was for a time pop-pop-pop—and then a whole volley; but when the regulars fired it seemed like one sheet of flame from right to left. Oh it was beautiful!"[147] The militia did its job well. Each man apparently fired at least once and some as many as five times and then began to withdraw when the British bayonets came in close, just as the plan called for. The British apparently tried to charge at least twice and were turned back by the accuracy and volume of the rifle fire from the militia. In all, the militia had delayed Tarleton's force for a little longer than a half an hour and had weakened the enemy considerably.

Morgan's well-crafted plan began to unravel slightly at this point. He had intended the militia to retreat around the left of Howard's main line, but instead they retreated around both sides of, and in many cases through, the main line. In the heat of battle, these men had acquitted themselves well, but the nuances of Morgan's plan were lost in a hail of lead and gleaming bayonets. Some of the militia broke and ran, running diagonally across the

View from the Patriot militia line that faced Tarleton's left.

front of the Continentals. Many of the militia were undoubtedly making for their horses in the rear to carry them as fast as possible away from the battle. James Collins, whom we heard from at Kings Mountain, and on the militia line, was one of the ones not just retreating but in headlong flight.

Tarleton saw exactly what he wanted to see, militia fleeing the battlefield, and decided to press his attack. His infantry was meeting the main line, and he then sent a detachment of fifty dragoons into the fleeing militia to scatter them. James Collins had a feeling that he was doomed when Tarleton's dragoons bore down on them. "Just as we got to our horses, they overtook us and began to make a few hacks at some."[148] While the infantry could not see this melee from their stations on the hill, William Washington spotted the action and took his American dragoons to deal with Tarleton's cavalry. Collins witnessed this fight during his flight to find his horse. "Col. Washington's cavalry was among them like a whirlwind, and the poor fellows began to keel from their horses without being able to remount. The shock was so sudden and so terrible that they could not stand it and immediately betook themselves to flight."[149]

Tarleton's infantry seemed to be winning the day up to this point, even if the dragoons had been beaten back. The British infantry had seemingly scattered Morgan's militia and now were in a full-fledged firefight with the Continentals on the main line. In Tarleton's memoirs he stated, "The fire on both sides was well supported and produced much slaughter."[150] As they traded volleys at close range, the British momentum ground to halt. As the fight progressed, the British line began to lengthen and overlap the flank of the Continentals as the Seventy-first Highlanders finally entered the fight. Howard did the logical thing and ordered the flank refused.[151] This meant that the end companies were to turn their front 90 degrees and face the new enemy threat. There was one of those mix-ups that seem to happen only at crucial moments in a battle, and the end companies actually refused their front, which meant that they turned 180 degrees, in effect mounting a retreat. When the other units on the main line saw this happening, they believed that they had missed an order and likewise began to move toward the rear. The Continental main line was withdrawing and threatened to create a rout if it were not checked. Morgan rode furiously up to Howard for an explanation, which Howard did not have. Howard did have the presence of mind, though, to inform Morgan that the Continentals were withdrawing in good order and definitely were not whipped. Morgan then designated a spot to the rear where he wished the main line to reform.[152] Howard rode with the men, and when Morgan demonstrated where he wanted the line

Double Envelopment at Cowpens

Green River Road as it runs roughly north–south through Morgan's Continental line.

The Washington Light Infantry monument and location of the linear firefight between the Continentals and Tarleton's infantry.

Area at which Colonel Howard's misunderstood order resulted in the Continentals retreating.

reformed, Howard exclaimed, "Stand and fire, men! Just one more volley. Old Morgan's never been whipped."[153]

The mistake in changing front was embarrassing for the Continentals and especially Howard, but it would prove to be fatal for Tarleton's designs that day. The British and their leader now saw exactly what they had anticipated before the battle began. The militia had seemingly fled, and the demoralized and out-flanked Continentals were in full retreat. Tarleton had to be thinking that this was a repeat of the Battle of Camden, and all that was left was to swoop in and finish the Americans off. All was not well in the British ranks, however, and Tarleton's infantry began to break formation and charge pell-mell into the Continentals in an attempt to rout them.

The Continental line followed Howard's instructions precisely, and according to Howard, "In a minute we had a perfect line."[154] They wheeled about, formed into a line of battle and fired into the British infantry. This British infantry just happened to be part of the one unit that was composed mainly of raw recruits, and now they found out that the battle was not won and were taking casualties at an alarming rate. Howard again described the fighting: "Our men commenced a very destructive fire, which they little expected, and a few rounds occasioned great disorder in their ranks."[155] It was the British turn to recoil in panic, and Howard sensed that he had an opportunity to break the British infantry.[156] Tarleton's army now faced a command-control crisis in its ranks. Many of the most experienced officers had been killed or wounded, and the remaining officers were on the verge of losing control of the men. Howard then ordered an extremely well-timed bayonet charge against the British infantry units. Here and there pockets of British infantry were still lunging at the Continentals, though, in the forlorn belief that one more charge would carry the day.

Washington had seen the events that had transpired and sent word to Morgan to "[g]ive them one more fire and I will charge them."[157] The cavalry would hit the British in the flank after the Continentals had delivered a volley. Howard's men fired a volley at point-blank range and then charged with bayonets. At this point, Tarleton had ordered his last dragoons forward to seal the victory, and they arrived roughly at the time of Howard's volley. Washington's cavalry ploughed into the British flank and sent the dragoons and nearby infantry into a state of wild disorder. The British front began to

View of the hill on which General Morgan and Colonel Howard reformed the Continentals.

121

disintegrate from this unexpected envelopment on their right and the bayonet charge in their front. Thomas Young presents a compelling description of this event: "The British broke, and throwing down their guns and cartouche boxes, made for the wagon road, and did the prettiest sort of running!"[158]

As if on cue, the militia had reformed, hit and overlapped the British in their left flank at almost the same moment. James Collins was with the militia, which earlier had retreated behind the Continentals, and according to his account, "By this time both lines of infantry was warmly engaged, and we being relieved from the pursuit of the enemy began to rally and prepare to redeem our credit, when Morgan rode up in front and waving his sword and cried out 'Form, form my brave fellows! Old Morgan was never beaten!'"[159] On the left, the British were thrown into severe disorder when unexpectedly engaged by the militia. James Collins witnessed the British line break as the militia hit them: "We then advanced briskly and gained the right flank of the enemy [the Continental left], and they, being hard pressed in front by Howard and falling very fast, could not stand it long. They began to throw down their arms and surrender themselves as prisoners of war."[160] The Americans had succeeded in an improbable double envelopment of the British; both flanks had been overlapped and broken, and the infantry almost completely routed.

The question will always linger: was the double envelopment by Morgan's design or was it a lucky occurrence? Morgan had promised the militia that they only had to fire three times, and then they would be protected by the bayonets of the Continentals. James Collins stated that Morgan and Pickens did indeed ride to the militia and encourage them to return to the fight—this at a moment when the contest was still in doubt. Dr. Lawrence Babits, in his groundbreaking 1998 book *A Devil of a Whipping*, agrees with James Collins that Morgan and Pickens were there to rally the militia. However, Lieutenant Colonel Jon Moncure in his earlier *Cowpens Staff Ride and Battlefield Tour* takes a different approach and posits that Howard or Washington could have sent a runner to request the militia or that Pickens could have simply made the maneuver of his own accord.[161] No matter what or who actually instigated the militia's return, it had a decidedly profound and devastating effect on the British.

Tarleton is perhaps our best witness to the effect of the envelopments on his army. The Americans, "taking advantage of the present situation, advanced upon the British troops, and augmented their astonishment. A general flight ensued."[162] Tarleton always had a bad habit of shifting blame to others and glossing over his failures, so the phrase "A general flight ensued" speaks volumes about the disorder of the British retreat. Tarleton was not going to give up the game so easily, though, and ordered his cavalry to reform and charge, or at least stave off, the Continentals and American dragoons while he tried to rally the infantry to protect his artillery. Tarleton again provides us with the details: "The cavalry did not comply with the order, and the effort to collect the infantry was ineffectual: Neither promises nor threats could gain their attention; they surrendered or dispersed."[163] Again, it is telling that Tarleton would admit in his memoirs that the cavalry refused an order and the infantry could not be reformed and many surrendered. The impact of the double envelopment had been absolutely devastating to Tarleton's army. His men had broken and would not obey the commands of the officers; this was the very definition of an army that had been routed.

Even at this late stage of the fight, Tarleton was not ready to admit defeat. Tarleton ordered cavalry from one of his elite regular units, the Seventeenth Light Dragoons, to form around him and charge the Americans.[164] Tarleton believed that a heavy cavalry charge would break the Americans, as their lines had become ragged in their bayonet charge against his infantry. Fourteen officers and forty enlisted men were all that would answer his call, hardly a heavy cavalry charge in anyone's book. According to Tarleton, "Above two hundred dragoons forsook their leader, and left the field of battle."[165] He charged with them into the oncoming Americans. Tarleton claims that his men drove Washington's cavalry back into the main line. If this were so, then no one except Tarleton has made any written mention of the fact. Capturing Tarleton was a prize that would finish off the battle in glorious fashion. As Washington was helping round up prisoners, he noticed the remaining British dragoons and believed that Tarleton would be found among them. Washington ordered a pursuit, and he himself was far out in front of the American cavalry. Unfortunately for Washington, only a few of his men heard the order and followed him.[166]

Tarleton himself had to ride like a madman to escape capture by Washington's dragoons. Tarleton was running from the field like he had seen the Patriots do numerous times. His horse initially was shot out from under him, and a kind British surgeon lent Tarleton his mount. William Washington and a few dragoons gave chase to Tarleton and his stalwart band that attempted the last futile charge. As they rode at breakneck speed, Tarleton and two of his men suddenly turned to give battle. He and Washington actually fought with each other for a moment, with Tarleton wounding Washington's horse with a pistol shot. Historian Thomas Fleming states that Washington actually headed straight for Tarleton to exact revenge for losses earlier in the war, and this description is perfectly logical, especially in light of American hatred of Tarleton.[167] During the engagement, Washington was surrounded by some of Tarleton's men, but the Americans had the advantage, and he extricated himself from the situation when a black soldier (or servant, depending on the account) shot one of the British cavalrymen who had engaged Washington.[168]

Tarleton eventually reached his baggage wagons, from which the guard had fled, using the wagon horses. The wagons themselves were in the road and were being looted by local Loyalists who had lately been employed as spies and guides. Tarleton and his men rode into the looters and killed several before the looters ran off.[169] It is not known whether Tarleton believed the looters were Patriots or if in fact he knew they were Loyalists. Tarleton then spent a short time burning or otherwise destroying what remained of the baggage lest it fall into American hands. Washington's dragoons pursued Tarleton and his little band for about twenty miles but were unable to overtake them. Washington's men happened to take the wrong road from the Cowpens, which enabled Tarleton to make good on his escape.

Back on the battlefield, Tarleton's Seventy-first Highlanders were trying to put together an orderly retreat. The Continentals and militia were making this task impossible since they were on the flank and the rear of the battalion remnant. The Highlanders attempted to form into a compact body and retreat in an orderly manner for a short time but were soon sent into disorder like the rest of the British infantry. Up to this point they had maintained order in their ranks, but the continued fire of the Continentals threw them into confusion. Most of the Highlanders threw down their arms and surrendered, seeing that Tarleton's dragoons and the remainder of the army had forsaken them and that they were virtually surrounded.[170] The last of the British left fighting were the artillerymen manning the two cannons. They continued to fight until all but one were shot or bayoneted.[171] The cavalry and infantry had broken and run, but Tarleton's artillerists had fought, literally, to the last man.

Just as at Kings Mountain, surrendering was not the simple exercise that the rules of war describe. Morgan's army was made up of groups who had fought at Kings Mountain, weathered the defeat at Camden, fought the Loyalists and British in the Carolinas backcountry and seen firsthand Tarleton's atrocities. Cries of "Give them Tarleton's Quarter!" rang out among the men to great cheers. Unlike at Kings Mountain, where the commanders were unable to control ill-disciplined militia, here at the Cowpens, Morgan and his senior officers got their men under control and granted the British quarter. A dark chapter in American history was avoided by this honorable act. There would be no repeat of the aftermath of Kings Mountain.

Tarleton's defeat was utter: his infantry had been routed, his cavalry grown cowardly and refused to obey commands, his tactics were parried and bested and his entire force was in danger of capture. By 9:00 a.m., Daniel Morgan had cracked his metaphorical whip over Benny Tarleton. Tarleton himself got away and lived to fight against the Americans on other fields, but on January 17, 1781, he was dealt a crippling blow that shattered his once-vaunted Legion and forced Cornwallis into a series of rash acts. Morgan was said to be so ecstatic in his victory that he literally picked up a nearby drummer boy and kissed him on both cheeks.

In totaling up the defeat, it is wise to look at the casualty figures. Morgan stated that his losses were "inconsiderable, not having more than twelve killed and sixty wounded."[172] These figures are absolutely astonishing in light of the fighting that was done by Morgan's army at the Cowpens. Morgan goes on to list the British losses in the battle, "10 commissioned officers and over 100 rank and file killed."[173] These figures give Morgan's army a kill ratio of almost ten to one, a feat that few armies have ever matched on any field. Tarleton's losses in wounded were reported in excess of 200 men of all ranks. Tarleton himself corroborates these statistics to a certain degree: "The number of killed and wounded, in the action at the Cowpens, amounted to near three hundred on both sides, officers and men inclusive."[174] While this matches Morgan's claims, Tarleton goes on to state, "This loss was almost equally shared," which the records show to be patently untrue.[175] In addition to subjecting the British to heavy casualties, Morgan captured more than 525 prisoners, a figure that Tarleton rounded down to "near four hundred prisoners" in his memoirs.[176]

There were many prizes of battle that came to Morgan as a result of his victory. He gained the two brass cannons, over eight hundred muskets, a traveling forge, a number of wagons, "seventy negroes" and more than one hundred horses for the dragoons.[177] The seventy Negroes were freed slaves that the British had brought along to act as servants for the officers, and one has to wonder how "free" they actually were. In addition to these larger items, there was a great amount of captured ammunition that Morgan distributed to the militia, clothing and other accoutrement from the British knapsacks that the men appropriated for themselves. The Patriots reaped a harvest of spoils from their victory.

Chapter 12
AFTERMATH OF COWPENS

Morgan did not savor his victory at the Cowpens for long. Morgan biographer Don Higginbotham posed the most serious question facing Morgan immediately after the battle: could he preserve his victory by escaping from Cornwallis?[178] Morgan believed that Cornwallis would be hot on his trail, especially once word of the magnitude of Tarleton's defeat reached him. The full weight of Cornwallis's main army would be brought to bear on Morgan's small force if they remained at the Cowpens, so rapid movement was essential. As a result of this perceived threat, he planned a hasty withdrawal from the Cowpens northward into North Carolina toward the Catawba River. Defeating Tarleton's reinforced Legion was one thing; fighting the main force of the British army would be suicide. Morgan also did not want Cornwallis to rescue the prisoners since this would be a huge boost to British fortunes in the very area that Morgan was being forced to vacate. In the meantime, Morgan sent patrols to locate the exact position of Cornwallis's army and determine the speed at which it was traveling.

By early afternoon, Morgan had his army up and on the move. Pickens's militia was left under a flag of truce to bury the dead and help with the wounded. A large portion of the militia was disbanded on the battlefield by their commanders that afternoon. We will likely never know the numbers involved as accurate records for the militia were not kept. Morgan marched northward and camped for the evening on the north side of the Broad River at Island Ford near modern Cliffside, North Carolina.[179] Morgan set a pace that matched, if not exceeded, his march to the Cowpens in the days leading to the battle. By the night of January 18, he had reached Gilbert Town. Here Morgan split his force. A detachment of dragoons took the prisoners on one road, while he went by a different route with the rest of his army. The prisoners were of the opinion that Cornwallis was close at hand and would liberate them, so they marched as slowly as prudence allowed and slowed the column considerably.[180] Morgan split the force to guard against the entire army falling into Cornwallis's hands, and the Americans guarding the prisoners had to use the bayonet to keep them marching. In fact one observer described the Patriots as driving their prisoners like wild beasts.

In Cornwallis's camp on Turkey Creek, he began to learn about Tarleton's disaster on the evening of January 17 as stragglers arrived in his camp. Tarleton finally rode into camp the next day with the roughly two hundred dragoons who had left the field and refused the final order to charge. As Tarleton described the events of the battle, Cornwallis was leaning on his sword, and it eventually snapped under the pressure. Cornwallis's temper snapped as well, and he swore that he would liberate the prisoners Morgan had captured. Cornwallis started his army for the Cowpens the next morning to chase the elusive Morgan, but Morgan was not there. Cornwallis's army had been reinforced with Leslie's men but was too slow to keep pace with Morgan's swifter and lighter force. Nevertheless, Cornwallis gave chase and pursued Morgan toward the Catawba.

On January 19, Banastre Tarleton sent a letter to Daniel Morgan asking that the British prisoners be treated as prescribed by the rules of war. Morgan and his lieutenants must have found this letter somewhat hypocritical in light of the way that Tarleton treated the men trying to surrender at the Waxhaws. Tarleton, however, showed himself to be a shrewd individual in the way he phrased the letter.

> *Sir—The action of 17th instant having thrown into your hands a number of British Officers and Soldiers I primarily request of you that Attention and Humanity may be exhibited towards the Wounded Officers and Men, for whose assistance I now send a Flag, Doctor Stewart and the Surgeon's Mate of the Seventh Regt. I secondly desire you to inform me the Number and Inability of the Prisoners, which the Fortune of War has placed in your possession.*
>
> *P.S.—I have sent some money for the use of the prisoners.*[181]

Aftermath of Cowpens

Tarleton must have received word or heard accounts of the way that the prisoners were treated after Kings Mountain and how the Patriots forced them to purchase food and water. This letter would serve to forestall such events from happening again as well as appealed to Morgan's sense of honor.

Morgan wanted to get his army north of the Catawba River, where he would be in a position of relative safety and would possibly be in a position to combine with Greene's main force. By January 23, his men had crossed the icy river by marching over roads that became little more than quagmires during the day and frozen stiff by the intense cold at night. The prisoners and their guard finally rejoined Morgan's army at this point. Morgan had marched his men at the killing pace of twenty miles per day with an army that was ill clad and growing hungry. This feat in and of itself may be one of the most masterful of the war; Morgan had consistently out-distanced the main enemy field army that was determined to catch him. Morgan was well ahead of Cornwallis and had made good on his initial escape.

At his camp near Sherill's ford on the Catawba, Morgan could now take a breath, though his little army began to lose men as enlistments ran out and militia left the service. One group of militia was tasked with guarding the prisoners on to Salisbury, North Carolina, and eventually Winchester and Richmond, Virginia, during their march home. These were the ex-Continental Virginia militia whose enlistments were just about to expire. One has to wonder if Morgan chose them to escort the prisoners to exact a bit of revenge for their leaving his army at this crucial hour. Though Morgan was temporarily safe, his army was dwindling, and he was fearful of not having enough men to fight another battle. Morgan also was suffering the debilitating effects of his sciatica. He couldn't ride without pain shooting down his hip and legs, and at times he was confined to his tent while in camp. Morgan's body was simply giving out under the stress and strain of the campaign.

Morgan had done what many thought was impossible and not only defeated Tarleton and his vaunted Legion, but also outdistanced Cornwallis's pursuit. He won the first leg of the race away from Cowpens, his army was in relative safety and his prisoners were on their way to Salisbury and eventually to Richmond, safe from liberation by Cornwallis. The question now begs to be asked: why did Morgan win at the Cowpens? There are six major reasons for Morgan's splendid victory:

1. The ground where the battle was fought was chosen well for an in-depth defense.

2. Morgan's army was composed of experienced troops who were opposed by a number of raw British recruits.

3. Morgan played to the unique strengths of his army while Tarleton fought in his traditional headlong manner.

4. Morgan used superior battlefield tactics that amplified his army's fighting capabilities.

5. Morgan's army was relatively well rested while Tarleton's was nearing physical exhaustion.

6. Morgan was able to impose his will on Banastre Tarleton.

Many historians have derided the choice of ground where Morgan chose to fight Tarleton, but that very ground helped seal American success. The way the ground sloped helped to conceal the American dragoons, shielded the militia as they reformed and framed up the battlefield in such a way that the American flanks were well protected. Banastre Tarleton, in his memoirs after the war, still stated that

> [t]*he ground which General Morgan had chosen for the engagement, in order to cover his retreat to the Broad river, was disadvantageous for the Americans, and convenient for the British: An open wood was certainly as proper a place for action as Lieutenant-colonel Tarleton could desire.*[182]

Tarleton apparently was not aware that the gentle undulations and changes in the terrain were part of the equation that led to his undoing. He does have one salient point, however. Morgan chose the Cowpens for its proximity to the Broad in case of disaster. Had Tarleton gained the field, at least a portion of Morgan's army would have been able to ford the river and live to fight another day.

Tarleton, by contrast, was ignorant of the terrain over which he was to fight that morning. While Morgan was at the field well before his army and selected the exact location deliberately, Tarleton's only survey of the actual field came when his men marched out of the wood line on the southern edge of the field near daybreak. Not knowing the terrain features—such as swampy areas, hills and depressions—gave him an incomplete view of the field that led to a serious mismanagement of his forces.

Morgan stated, from the end of the battle until his death, that about eight hundred men comprised his army. This figure is probably six hundred or more men low, but no matter the number, they were hard-bitten veterans. These were men such as McDowell's North Carolina militia, who had savaged Ferguson at Kings Mountain, and the Maryland line that had stood its ground so well at Camden. These men had tasted battle before and had passed that ultimate test. The sights, sounds and smells of the battlefield would not be a shock to them as they could be to raw recruits. Tarleton's army, by contrast, had a number of untested recruits who had not seen hard combat before their baptism at the Cowpens. Though Tarleton did not seem to be concerned by this inexperience, when the Continentals on the main line suddenly reformed, fired a volley and charged with the bayonet, the recruits broke in confusion.

Daniel Morgan knew that he was in the fight of his life at the Cowpens; in fact, his statement about beating Tarleton at the spot or laying his bones indicated just that. One misstep in the battle could lead to a disaster, from which his army and the Patriot cause may not be able to recover. To avoid the fatal misstep, Morgan analyzed his options and formulated his plan based on the strengths of his available forces. The Continentals and Virginia militia were superb and could be counted on in a pinch, but their numbers were relatively few. Using them as the main line of resistance was possible only if the militia could delay and weaken Tarleton's force. Militia could not readily stand up to infantry, and asking them to do so was futile. Morgan's plan took this into account, as well as what the British thought they would see. Some militiamen were used to form a skirmish line that was designed to pick off men and anger Tarleton, a job at which they excelled. Then well-aimed fire of the militia, on the militia line, took out a number of officers and men and delayed Tarleton's infantry for almost a half-hour. The militia were allowed to retire, while the Continentals exchanged volleys with what remained of Tarleton's force. The American cavalry would form a highly mobile reserve, able to fight wherever on the battlefield they were needed. In short, Morgan fashioned a defense in-depth that could resist a classic British charge.

Tarleton, on the other hand, was not imaginative with his forces in virtually any way. He formed them in an almost straight line and charged them straight ahead at the American militia. He formed his men with only the Seventy-first Highlanders and a few dragoons as any sort of reserve, and they were in poor position to deliver a knockout blow once the battle began. His greatest strength was in the fighting prowess of the Legion and the Light Infantry. Instead of devising a sweeping cavalry strike or attempting to flank the Americans using the Light Infantry, Tarleton did what Morgan expected: he attacked head on. Loyalist Alexander Chesney, who caught up with

Tarleton the day before the battle, stated that the British "suffered a total defeat by some dreadful bad management."[183] This is a stinging indictment of Tarleton's tactical prowess from a man who had fought with Ferguson in the debacle at Kings Mountain.

Morgan not only devised a defense that played to the strengths of his army but also used innovative tactics at critical moments of the battle. In placing Washington's dragoons in reserve, Morgan had created a force that could see most of the field and respond as needed. Twice the dragoons would sweep aside Tarleton's men that had been sent on a pell-mell attack. Once they defeated the British cavalry that was harassing the retreating militia, they savaged the British infantry after the Continental line inadvertently did an about face. Morgan also used the mistaken order that sent Howard's Continentals retreating to his advantage. Instead of ordering a general retreat, Morgan sought an appropriate place to reform and strike at the British. This unexpected strike staggered the enemy and helped break them. Lastly, Morgan used the militia to draw the British in via their planned withdrawal. The militia reforming and attacking the British in the front and flank was unexpected and created much disorder. These unique tactics stymied the British, and Tarleton was not able to effectively counter them on January 17.

Tarleton, on the other hand, was as innovative in his tactics as he was with his plan for the battle. Where Morgan had a defense in-depth, Tarleton aligned his infantry in a long line only two men deep. When the American line was pierced, the Patriots had reserves and other units to shore up the line. In the thin British line, if it were pierced, the line was essentially broken and difficult to reform. Tarleton admits his deployment was a mistake but gives his requisite disclaimer as to fault. He attributed the problem to

> the loose manner of forming which had always been practised by the King's troops in America...The extreme extension of the files always exposed the British regiments and corps, and would, before this unfortunate affair, have been attended with detrimental effect, had not the multiplicity of lines with which they generally fought rescued them from such imminent danger.[184]

Tarleton simply states that his men did not form up as they should and of course that the enemy didn't fight in the correct manner. One has to wonder what the job of a commander in the British army was, in Tarleton's opinion, if it were not to see that such things were corrected. Tarleton, as mentioned before, has a penchant for laying blame on others, and this description is a classic example. The field at the Cowpens is simply too narrow to have allowed a loose formation as he describes to form on the field. The line may have, in reality, been only two men deep, but that line could not have physically been as loose as he describes, or else they would have been posted in a swampy area and in a creek well away from the main fighting. The tactics that Tarleton chose to employ at the Cowpens helped bring about his defeat at the hands of Daniel Morgan.

Morgan's march through the South Carolina backcountry produced a decidedly deleterious effect on Tarleton's men. The pace that Morgan set, and hence the pace that Tarleton forced his army to match, was such that it would physically exhaust the hardiest of men. Morgan instructed his men to block roads, set up minor ambushes and do everything in their power to retard Tarleton in his pursuit. This forced Tarleton to not only keep his men on the move, but also compel them to stop and start often during the day and move out in formation to clear possible ambush positions. This type of movement is taxing on an army's strength, and Tarleton's was no exception. While Tarleton only averaged around thirteen miles per day, they were thirteen mentally taxing and physically backbreaking miles. Add to the equation the scant rations that the British were provided before the march, and physical exhaustion begins to set in. The British were not given enough calories to recover from the physical exertions they were required to make, and the area had been picked clean of provisions by Morgan's army days before. In fact, Tarleton's remark about finding good provisions at Morgan's hastily abandoned camp provides a clue to the supply situation in his ranks. The result was that Tarleton's men were physically exhausted, which led them to the edge of mental exhaustion. On January 17, they were awake and on the march at 3:00 a.m. and went straight into the attack when they got to the Cowpens at daybreak. When the British were faced with accurate rifle fire and the fatal mirage of the Continental retreat, it was more than soldiers could stand.

Lastly, Morgan was able to virtually impose his will on Tarleton by making him think what Morgan wanted him to think and see what Morgan wanted him to see. Morgan retreated very fast from his Pacolet camp toward the Broad. This hasty movement gave Tarleton the illusion that Morgan was on the run (whether he actually was or not), and Tarleton wanted to run him to ground. Morgan was gathering reinforcements along the way, something Tarleton discovered only the day before the battle. Morgan led Tarleton through an area that had been picked clean of supplies and forced him to set a killing pace in order to keep up. All of this weakened

Tarleton's men before the battle even began. Morgan turned to fight at an unexpected time, and to Tarleton it was a desperate, last-ditch defense by a scared army. Little did he suspect the trap that lay in wait for him; all he saw was an enemy forcing a march to get across the Broad to safety. Finally, Morgan used his militia to encourage Tarleton to attack and, when he obliged, used his militia to show Tarleton what he wanted to see: the militia fleeing. Morgan had Tarleton doing exactly what he wanted, and that never bodes well for a commander to be forced to do the opponent's bidding, either by circumstance or subterfuge.

Militarily, Daniel Morgan out-generalled Banastre Tarleton on the plains of the Cowpens. From the moment Tarleton began his pursuit of Morgan through the South Carolina backcountry to the last cavalry charge of the battle, Morgan was ahead of Banastre Tarleton. Morgan was quoted as saying, "[I]f men are forced to fight, they will sell their lives dearly." His men did so in the short campaign that culminated at the Cowpens. His design of the battle, his leadership of the men, his coolness under attack and his ability to improvise in the face of uncertainty created a situation that Tarleton could not effectively counter. Tarleton, on the other hand, was so sure of himself and his army that he did not bother with the nuances of planning the battle or dictating tactics. When the tide of battle turned against him, Tarleton was unable to make the adjustments necessary to secure victory or in the end to stave off defeat.

Another question that needs to be asked is what did Morgan really accomplish at the Cowpens. Roger Lamb left an excellent account of his service in the king's army during the American Revolution. According to Lamb:

> *This defeat (particularly the loss of the light infantry) was a severe loss to the royal camp. The prisoners were conveyed by forced marches to Richmond; so that all attempts of the main army to re-capture them were unavailing. The army halted during two days collecting provisions and destroying superfluous baggage. We then marched through North Carolina, to the banks of the Dan, on to the utmost extremities of the province.*[185]

Morgan virtually destroyed Cornwallis's only remaining unit of light troops. The loss of these troops would prove to be critical as the campaign through North Carolina and into Virginia ground on. Combine the loss of the light troops with the way the battle inspired, or "spirited up," the people, and Cornwallis had a disaster on his hands. As word reached Richmond and Philadelphia, toasts were given in Morgan's honor, and proclamations were written. The victory had lifted the Patriot cause at a time when fortunes had again been sagging and prospects for independence looked dim. The only way for Cornwallis to reverse the Cowpens disaster was to quickly bring Morgan to battle and destroy his force. Cornwallis's army was not quick enough to do so in the days after the battle, nor was it able to gather effective intelligence about where Morgan's army was or what direction it was headed. Morgan secured the most elusive of victories at the Cowpens: his army destroyed Tarleton's reinforced Legion as a fighting force, the people of the area and the country were electrified and he made good on his escape.

Cornwallis was infuriated at losing the race to the Catawba River. Morgan's army, even though encumbered with the spoils of war and prisoners, had been able to outpace him each step of the way. The only way Cornwallis could deal with Morgan on anything like equal speed was to use his light forces. The problem was that the light forces had been destroyed—Ferguson at Kings Mountain and Tarleton at the Cowpens. Only those dragoons who left the field at Cowpens were available to carry out the scouting, gathering intelligence and dealing with militia that the light infantry and Legion had formerly done.

Cornwallis made a difficult, and in the end fatal, decision and tried to turn his whole army into a light force. After reaching the Catawba at Ramsour's Mill and finding that Morgan had already passed, Cornwallis ordered all of the excess baggage burned. This meant extra wagons, clothing, accoutrement, supplies and even the rations of rum. Cornwallis went so far as to throw his own belongings into the blaze to show how serious he was about the matter, and his officers did the same. While discarding the items that slowed his army down would indeed make it faster, Cornwallis was setting his army up to be unable to resupply, refit or support itself in an extended campaign. The infantry would no longer sleep in tents and would have to supply themselves through foraging in the countryside, and the officers would not have the relatively comfortable existence that they had known thus far. The army would travel light, live in the field and move rapidly to intercept Morgan. General Clinton had earlier ordered Cornwallis to restrain from a second invasion of North Carolina, but Cornwallis was intent on catching Morgan and destroying his army. By the beginning of February, Cornwallis was ready to cross the Catawba and continue his pursuit. According to British soldier Roger Lamb, "On the 1st day of February, at day light in the morning we were directed to cross M'Cowan's Ford."[186]

Nathanael Greene made a long journey through the North Carolina countryside to meet with Morgan at his camp near the Catawba. The decision was made to try and unite the two parts of the southern army to oppose Cornwallis. The British had been seriously weakened at the Cowpens, and drawing them farther from their bases in South Carolina might provide the combined southern army with a chance to deal Cornwallis a serious blow. That blow would come at the end of a long and torturous march that would see both armies range far and wide.

Chapter 13

RACE TO THE DAN

The campaign took a decidedly different turn after the initial march to
the Catawba. Morgan had Nathanael Greene in camp, and both men
decided that they could hold the fords of the Catawba with the forces that
they had available. The decision to hold the Catawba fords was based on
three factors. One was that holding the fords would allow the prisoners to get
far enough away from Cornwallis as to be beyond his reach. Secondly, the
main force of the southern army was marching hard to join Morgan's flying
army and together oppose Cornwallis. The last was that even if they were
unable to stop Cornwallis from crossing the Catawba, he would be delayed
long enough for the prisoners to make good their march northward and give
the main force time to hopefully effect a junction.

There were two major rivers that would have to be crossed by Cornwallis
in order to catch Morgan, the Catawba and the Yadkin. The winter weather
that had turned the roads into a soupy mess also served to raise the rivers well
above their normal levels. Morgan and Greene made the decision to dispute
the Catawba crossings but had different plans in mind for the Yadkin. The
Yadkin was so high that boats were necessary to effect a safe crossing. If
Cornwallis were to reach the Yadkin, Morgan's men would gather all of the
boats in the area and, after crossing themselves, would sabotage them so the
British could not cross the river. Greene and Morgan, in effect, were using
the two rivers as natural fortifications to fight a delaying action behind.

Unfortunately, Cornwallis was successful in fording the Catawba on
February 1, after the water had fallen low enough for a crossing. General

Davidson of the North Carolina militia was killed at Cowan's Ford in the process of defending the crossing site. Morgan had wisely designated a place for the militia units to retreat to in the event of Cornwallis crossing the river. His belief was that the units would meet at this spot and continue on to Salisbury with the Continentals and the rest of the army. Many militia units decided that it was time to leave the field, and instead of rallying at the designated location, they continued their march homeward.[187]

Cornwallis was facing an even greater challenge than the swollen rivers and lack of transportation across them. His army was attempting to live off of the land in an area that was decidedly hostile. In the summer and fall of 1780, Cornwallis's army had experienced some success at gathering food and forage in the Carolina backcountry, but by the late winter of 1781, the situation was quite different. Morgan's army had already stripped the area clean of supplies and there was very little left for the British to scrounge. This created a situation in Cornwallis's army where men were compelled to extreme exertion while receiving too few calories and too little nutrients to maintain their strength. The old military adage that an army travels on its stomach is quite true, and this lack of food led to decreases in physical strength and stamina, as well as lowered morale in the British ranks.

The inhabitants of this part of North Carolina were very fearful of the approach of Cornwallis and his army. The British were known to burn the houses of everyone in their path who was a Patriot and any home in which the man of the house was not present to prove that he was not with the Patriot militia. As a result, a number of families packed up what belongings they could and marched in the rear of Morgan's army.[188] Morgan spent precious time ferrying these refugees across the Yadkin, so much so that Cornwallis's lead elements were in proximity when the last of the civilians crossed.[189] When Cornwallis's force reached the Yadkin, he found a raging and impassable waterway. Indeed, he would have to use boats to cross the river in its present state, yet Morgan's men had either stolen, hidden or sabotaged them all. Cornwallis's only option was to wait until the river went down enough that he could get his men across. Greene and Morgan continued to be able to outpace Cornwallis toward Guilford Court House (modern Greensboro, North Carolina).

During this period of the campaign, Morgan's sciatica (or possibly a bulging disk in his spine) was extremely inflamed, leaving him virtually crippled. He could not ride at more than a walk and in camp was almost confined to a cot. When the flying army arrived at Guilford Court House, the main force, temporarily under General Isaac Huger, joined them there.

Race to the Dan

At this point, Morgan felt like he had completed his immediate mission and asked Greene for leave to return home to Winchester. On February 6, he wrote to General Greene:

> *I am much indisposed with pains, and to add to my misfortunes, am violently attacked with the piles* [hemorrhoids], *so that I can scarcely sit upon my horse. This is the first time that I ever experienced this disorder, and from the idea I had of it, sincerely prayed that I might never know what it was.*[190]

Greene desperately wanted Morgan to stay with the army but knew that physically the campaign had taken its toll on Morgan. On February 10, Greene issued the following order, "Gen. Morgan, of the Virginia line, has leave of absence until he recovers his health, so as to be able to take the field again."[191] Greene went so far as to offer Morgan another independent command, this time of the North Carolina militia, to help keep him in the field, but Morgan had to decline due to his failing health. One of the most dynamic and successful Patriot leaders was leaving the field.

The campaign now entered its final phase as the combined southern army faced Cornwallis's Britons near Guilford Court House. Greene's army was in no condition for a general engagement with Cornwallis, so a retreat was his only option, and the North Carolina rivers would provide him with cover. Greene wanted to get his army across the Dan River and into Virginia and force Cornwallis to pursue him in that direction. On February 10, the main body of the southern army left Guilford Court House for the Dan, while a smaller detachment passed across the front of Cornwallis army. This move alarmed Cornwallis, who stopped his army in order to gather intelligence and determine the intentions of the Americans. This bold maneuver allowed Greene to gain a full day's march on Cornwallis and to outdistance him yet again. The race ended when Greene's army crossed the Dan on February 13 and 14, leaving Cornwallis on the south bank boiling with impotent rage.

The campaign would take yet another turn as both armies moved back into the Guilford Court House area in March and fought one of the largest battles of the southern campaign. At Guilford Court House, on March 15, 1781, Greene used the same basic tactics that Morgan used at Cowpens. His defense in-depth and Cornwallis's dedication to attacking created a field of carnage. Greene listed his casualties as 79 killed, 185 wounded and over 1,000 missing, well over a quarter of his army. Cornwallis reported 93 killed, 413 wounded and 26 missing, over a quarter of his army as well.

Cornwallis's army technically won the battle and actually took the field, but at a cost that his army was not able to afford. Another such pyrrhic victory would have ruined Cornwallis's army. Greene retreated southward after the battle, and in April 1781 Cornwallis abandoned the pursuit, looking for success in Virginia. Cornwallis later left Virginia and marched overland to Wilmington, North Carolina. In May 1781, he marched back to the hamlet of Petersburg, Virginia. Greene moved his army into South Carolina and harassed the British forces there for the remainder of the war.

The war would see its last major battle at Yorktown, Virginia, in October 1781. Cornwallis's tired, hungry and threadbare army had marched across three states in a vain attempt at subjugating the Patriot forces and the Patriot cause. In the end, Cornwallis was surrounded on the Yorktown peninsula by George Washington, who was able to slip his army from the north and surround Cornwallis with the aid of the French fleet. Britain's only viable field army had surrendered; a year and a half later Britain formally ceased hostilities and America was an independent nation. The road to victory started in the Carolinas backcountry and the stunningly complete victories at Kings Mountain and Cowpens.

Chapter 14

CONCLUSION

The Battles of Kings Mountain and Cowpens set into motion a chain of events that ended with Cornwallis's surrender at Yorktown. The effects of these two battles changed the fundamental dynamics of the war in the South and created an environment for the British to fail in their attempt to regain control of the colonies. The strategy and tactics of the Americans changed radically, and the British were either unable or unwilling to effectively respond. The military mistakes of the British would in the end be their undoing. The Battle of Kings Mountain was the archetype for those who see the Revolution as Americans in hunting shirts and buckskin fighting with their long rifles against a well-trained European style enemy. While these characteristics are not completely correct, there is a tremendous amount truth in them. The Battle of Cowpens, on the other hand, was fought with a balance of flexibility and military precision rarely encountered on the battlefield. These two very different engagements left the king's cause in America battered and bruised and ultimately were fatal to it.

First and foremost, at Kings Mountain, Cornwallis lost one of his two elite light units. Ferguson's corps of Loyalist militia was destroyed, with the vast majority either killed or captured. The British army had come to rely on such units to range far and wide from the main army to gather intelligence and to deal with Patriot militia units. After the battle at Kings Mountain, Cornwallis had lost half of his light forces, which left the Legion to do the job two units had previously done. To further complicate matters, the intense militia activity in the area immediately around Charlotte forced Cornwallis to guard all of his foraging parties and express mail couriers lest they end up captured or killed. This requirement placed a strain on the Legion and other units of Cornwallis's army and wore down the fighting efficiency of the Legion and other mounted troops at a time when they would be sorely needed.

Ferguson's defeat at Kings Mountain practically forced Cornwallis to abandon Charlotte, North Carolina, as his base of operations and ended his invasion of the state. With the destruction of Ferguson's corps, Cornwallis's left flank was vulnerable to attack by militia groups such as the ones who fought at Kings Mountain. The militia activity in the area had reached a fever pitch with foraging parties and couriers being attacked on a regular basis. The supply and communications lines to Charleston were long, slow and hard to defend, and resupplying the army out off of the local countryside was becoming increasingly problematic. With the actions of the local militia, the nearly constant problems of supplying the army, and his now vulnerable left flank, caused Cornwallis to move his army south to Winnsboro, South Carolina, for the winter. This placed him closer to his base of supply and allowed his army to help reinforce and protect vulnerable outposts throughout the area.

The Battle of Kings Mountain also severely hurt the morale of the Loyalists in the area. From the moment that Charleston fell, the Patriot cause in South Carolina had suffered defeat after defeat. The Battle of Camden, in particular, had facilitated a nadir in Patriot prospects for slowing Cornwallis on his march of conquest. A number of militia actions such as Williamson's Plantation (also known as Huck's Defeat) and Musgrove's Mill were Patriot victories over British units, but they were all small affairs and their effect on morale was local at best. At Kings Mountain, though, the Patriot militia units combined en masse to defeat an elite Loyalist force and succeeded in removing it from the military equation. The size and nature of the Kings Mountain victory was devastating to the Loyalist morale. Ferguson had been sent to suppress the Patriots and cow them into submission to the crown, but his army had been soundly defeated and he had been killed in the process. Instead of throngs of Loyalists rallying to the cause, Cornwallis was met with a lukewarm reception at best. The Loyalists of the backcountry were fearful of reprisals at the hands of their Patriot neighbors and Patriot militia if they joined Cornwallis or expressed and allegiance to the Crown. The result was that the expected multitudes of Loyalists failed to turn out for Cornwallis.

Conclusion

Lastly, the Patriot victory at Kings Mountain emboldened the Patriots and led to an increase in partisan activity in the Carolinas, especially in the backcountry. After the battle and Ferguson's defeat, Patriot leaders such as Francis Marion and Thomas Sumter, once he recuperated from his wounds, stepped up operations aimed at retarding Cornwallis's advance. The formerly seemingly unbeatable British army had been stymied by an irregular group of militia who had destroyed a significant portion of Cornwallis's fighting strength. This led to militia units turning out and moving to key points such as Charlotte or joining leaders such as Marion and Sumter. As the Patriot ranks swelled, so did their operations, especially in areas formerly held by Cornwallis's army.

The Battle of Kings Mountain had forced Cornwallis to abandon his invasion of North Carolina, and he harbored a desire to move back into the state. However, when Nathanael Greene split the American southern army and sent Morgan and his corps out to harass the left flank of Cornwallis, it forced Cornwallis to send Tarleton to deal with the threat. After the defeat of Tarleton and his reinforced Legion, it caused Cornwallis's temper to boil over and give Morgan chase. Cornwallis had to catch and destroy Morgan's army in order to have any hope of reversing the disaster that Tarleton's battle had been. This meant that he had to put his army on the road and pursue an enemy in Morgan who had shown time and again that he could outpace almost any conventional force. General Clinton had ordered Cornwallis to remain in South Carolina and solidify the king's presence there, but Cornwallis chose to ignore this order and set off after Morgan. This headlong flight to catch Morgan put an extreme amount of wear and tear on his army that would be crucial in the coming campaign. Cornwallis's impetuous chase to redeem his military reputation would have dire consequences as the campaign entered a new phase, with an army that was tired, threadbare and worn out.

The Patriot victory at Cowpens had a major impact on the spirit of the people. One of Greene's goals for Morgan when he set out from the main army was to "spirit up the people of the area," and his victory had done just that. From the backwater of South Carolina to the halls of Congress in Philadelphia, Patriot morale improved. Morgan had taken a small group of Continentals, supplemented them with local militia and had defeated the vaunted Banastre Tarleton, destroying his Legion and sending the remaining dragoons to flight. Men drank toasts to Morgan's health, and the Congress voted he and his commanders medals and swords. General William Davidson, commander of the North Carolina militia, sent the following to Morgan on January 22: "Your victory over Tarleton has gladdened every countenance in this part. We had a Feu de Joy in consequence of it."[192] In a congratulatory letter to Morgan, General Otho Williams, the southern army's adjutant general, stated, "The advantages you have gained are important and do great Honor to your little Corps. We have had a feu de joy, drank all your Healths, Swear you are the finest fellows, and love you if possible more than ever."[193] What had been a period of darkness and desolation had given way to optimism and hope.

Arch-Loyalist Alexander Chesney stated in his journal that "[t]he Rebels increased much in the neighborhood…and a general rising being expected, I sent express for Col. Balfour the commandant of Charles-town to acquaint him of it."[194] General Otho Williams relayed the following as a postscript in his letter to Morgan: "Yesterday the famous Major Gray, the infamous spy and notorious horse thief, lost his mulatto Head. It is exhibited at Cheraw Hill, a terror to Tories."[195] The backcountry of South Carolina would again experience the type of civil war that had been so prevalent since the initial British victory at Charleston.

New militia units took to the field to replace those who were about to leave the service or who were to return to their home area. Governor Rutledge wrote Morgan from his exile in North Carolina about the victory at Cowpens: "It will excite many to emulate their Patriotism, & by the undaunted Courage and Perseverance of Freemen who are determined to maintain the Independence of America, that must (with the Blessing of God on our Arms) be firmly established."[196] As Morgan moved north of the Catawba, more militia units joined him to replace those that had left the service. In fact, Morgan felt that he may possibly be able to hold the fords of the Catawba with the force he had available. As the march moved northward, Morgan and Greene's army would maintain its strength, while the army of Cornwallis would get progressively smaller and weaker with each passing day. The few Loyalists that rallied to the king's cause in North Carolina were not numerous enough to offset the losses that Cornwallis would experience in the course of the campaign.

The defeat at the Cowpens took the one remaining elite light force out of Cornwallis's army. The Legion had been the one force that Cornwallis could count on to scout ahead of the army, gather intelligence, scatter Patriot militia bands and secure his lines of supply and communications. The Legion had also proven in the prelude to Cowpens that they could keep up with the swift army of Morgan, bringing on the Battle of Cowpens due to their rapid pursuit. After the firing stopped on the morning of January 17, 1781, the reinforced Legion no longer existed as a fighting force. Cornwallis did not have a unit on which he could rely to scout or to chase a swift enemy. The main force was all that Cornwallis had left. General Leslie rode into camp on Turkey Creek the day after the Battle of Cowpens with his 1,500 reinforcements, but these reinforcements were regular infantry. As regular infantry, with the attendant wagons and baggage, slogged through the countryside, they were generally protected by light troops such as the Legion, but now they were on their own in the Carolina backcountry. Cornwallis no longer had more than a handful of dragoons to scour the countryside and fend off ambushes and other attacks while on the march.

The loss of his light units convinced Cornwallis to make one of his most fateful decisions of the campaign. He decided that his entire army would become a quasi-light force and would discard the impediments that had slowed them down. They would live off of the countryside, sleep outdoors and march swiftly to catch Morgan. While in theory Cornwallis's army would have been a faster and lighter force, in reality he rid himself of the very tools his army would need to properly refit and equip itself for a long campaign. The farther that his army marched through the North Carolina backcountry chasing Daniel Morgan, the weaker and less effective his army became. Never an army of overwhelming numerical advantage on most battlefields, Cornwallis would watch his army slowly dwindle due to combat deaths and injuries, sickness and desertion. While his army was weakening, Morgan and Greene's armies were maintaining their strength as militia units came and went with their requisite irregularity.

Lastly, the Battle of Cowpens showed the Patriot commanders, particularly Nathanael Greene, how to defeat Cornwallis's regulars with a combined force of Continentals and militia. There had been instances of the militia defeating a regular force in the Carolina backcountry—Williamson's Plantation, Musgrove's Mill, Blackstocks and even Kings Mountain—but none of these battles had the scale or military precision of Cowpens. The use of the skirmishers to initiate the battle, using the militia to target officers and seemingly retreat, the main line of resistance formed by the Continentals and using the dragoons as a mobile reserve were the rough pattern that Greene would use to bleed Cornwallis's army at Guilford Court House later in the war. Cornwallis's regulars were no longer seen as unbeatable on the field; they could be dealt with by a combined force and could be defeated if the battle was planned correctly and the men were led properly.

Individually, the Battles of Kings Mountain and Cowpens had profound effects; however, their effects were even more startling when viewed together. The synergism of the effects produced by these two battles resulted in a massive shift in the fortunes of the Patriot cause and ultimately doomed the British to defeat. Individually, the battles were of great importance in the war, but combined they created the overall environment necessary for American success.

Prior to the Battle of Kings Mountain in October 1780, the Patriot cause was at low ebb. Throughout South Carolina, Loyalists were coming out in significant numbers in support of the Crown. Reprisals and a bushwhacking civil war marked the backcountry. The British army now under Cornwallis seemed like an unstoppable force. Defeats at Camden, the massacre at the Waxhaws and the wounding of Thomas Sumter sent the Patriot cause reeling. There was no true American army left in the field to oppose Cornwallis or prevent his army from doing as it pleased. After the Battles of Kings Mountain and Cowpens, those fortunes irrevocably changed.

The victories at Kings Mountain and Cowpens raised the level of enthusiasm to new heights. The victories stymied the steamroller-like momentum that Cornwallis's army had developed over the course of the summer and early fall. The two battles showed that the vaunted British regulars could be beaten in the open field of combat. The British were also forced to, if not retreat, at least change their base of operations for the first time in the campaign and then to give chase to an enemy that was skilled at evading them. All of this helped give hope to a cause that had very little to be hopeful about in the late summer of 1780.

The Patriot victories at Kings Mountain and Cowpens created and supported an environment for more Patriot militia to take to the field. Successes such as the overwhelming victories at Kings Mountain and Cowpens bred the type of enthusiasm that drew men into the ranks. Even though this patriotic fever cooled in the area where Cornwallis subsequently invaded, it did help other units to take to the field in areas not threatened by his army. Instead of a seemingly unstoppable enemy, the British now seemed to have weaknesses that could be exploited by energetic and capable officers. As more men turned out to muster during the campaign, it encouraged increased partisan activity in the backcountry of the Carolinas. Areas where the British had only a thin presence were subject to the activities of Patriot leaders such as Sumter, Marion and Pickens. These groups instilled fear in the Loyalist population and maintained a quasi-military presence that discouraged Loyalists from rallying to the British cause or helping the British in any way. The insurgency that was stoked by the Battles of Kings Mountain and Cowpens was something that the British were either unwilling, or unable, to effectively deal with. As a result, the only areas that the British had any

Conclusion

real control over were ones where their troops were present or where there were large regular patrols. The remaining areas, which encompassed the vast majority of the Carolinas, were effectively under Patriot control.

The defeats at Kings Mountain and Cowpens bled Cornwallis's field army white. Never an extremely numerous force, the numbers of men killed, wounded and captured in these two battles represented a sizeable portion of Cornwallis's fighting strength. The two battles alone represent an elimination of almost two thousand fighting men, many of them the elite of the British army. Among those killed or captured were many of the best unit level officers, and Ferguson himself was one of the best organizers and trainers in the army. Without experienced and skilled leadership, Cornwallis's army could not be expected to perform at a high level in the engagements that were to follow. General Leslie arrived at Cornwallis's Turkey Creek camp a little while after Cowpens, and his reinforcements appeared to offset the losses at Kings Mountain and Cowpens. Simply looking at numbers can be deceiving, however. The casualties in both battles included the vast majority of the two elite light forces that Cornwallis had available. Leslie's men added numbers, but the numbers they added were regular heavy infantry, the exact type that could not keep up with Morgan when Cornwallis initially chased him to the Catawba. The fighting power, combat effectiveness and sheer size of Cornwallis's army had been irreparably damaged as a result of the two key battles in the Carolinas backcountry.

The engagements at Kings Mountain and Cowpens took the strategic initiative away from Cornwallis and put it in the hands of the Patriots. While not clearly visible to some of the officers or leaders at the time, Cornwallis would be forced to react to Patriot actions rather than executing designs of his own. Cornwallis's retreat into upper South Carolina, splitting the army and sending Tarleton to deal with Morgan, the decision to give chase to Morgan and lastly the decision to turn the entire field army into a light fighting force were attempts to parry Patriot actions. Cornwallis would still conduct operations in the Carolinas backcountry, but he would not do so without weighing the intentions of the Patriots or guarding against their possible movements. Cornwallis would be forced to detach more men for garrison and guard duty than he wished due to the increased partisan and militia activity spawned by the Patriot victories.

The aftermath of the Battles of Kings Mountain and Cowpens saw Cornwallis change the focus of his campaign and forced him to operate in hostile territory. Initially, in the late summer of 1780, Cornwallis had been planning to invade North Carolina with his field army and hold South

Carolina with Loyalist militia. The defeat at Kings Mountain ended the first invasion and resulted in a change of base. During the ensuing winter of 1780–81, Cornwallis planned for a second invasion of North Carolina when the weather warmed and roads became passable. Greene, taking command of the American southern army and sending Morgan and his flying army into Cornwallis's flank and rear, changed that plan. Instead of Tarleton dealing Morgan a sound defeat, Cornwallis found himself invading North Carolina while chasing an enemy that left his army grasping at air. Instead of an invasion of conquest, Cornwallis was trying desperately to support his army in a hostile area while trying in vain to catch the elusive American army. Cornwallis retooled his whole army into one large light force in an attempt to catch Morgan and destroy him in a pitched battle.

While General Clinton said Kings Mountain was "[a]n event which was immediately productive of the worst consequences to the King's affairs in South Carolina, and unhappily the first link in a chain of evils that followed in regular succession until they at last ended in the loss of America," his analysis is less than perfect. The Battles of Kings Mountain and Cowpens together ignited the chain of events that ended in the loss of America. From the moment of the first fire on the ridges of Kings Mountain to the capture of Tarleton's artillery at Cowpens, the entire complexion of the war changed. The tide of the war turned, and what had been a seemingly easy campaign turned into ignominious defeat.

NOTES

CHAPTER 2

1. Gregory Urwin, "The War for Independence" presentation, U.S. History Consortium, Philadelphia, Pennsylvania, 2005.
2. Ibid.
3. Ibid.
4. Ibid.

CHAPTER 3

5. Don Higginbotham, *Daniel Morgan Revolutionary Rifleman* (Chapel Hill: University of North Carolina Press, 1961), 61.
6. Ibid., 64–66.
7. Battle of Saratoga History and Culture, National Park Service (Saratoga, New York), http://www.nps.gov/sara/historypculture/index.htm.
8. Ibid.
9. Higginbotham, *Daniel Morgan*, 92–99.
10. Bill Troppman, "Washington's Winter at Valley Forge" field study (Valley Forge, PA: U.S. History Consortium, 2005).

CHAPTER 4

11. William Gilmore Simms, *The Scout* (Chicago: Donohue Hennenberry & Co., 1890), 29.

12. Robert Dunkerly, *Kings Mountain Walking Tour Guide* (Pittsburgh: Dorrance, 2003), 9.
13. Dennis E. Frye, "The Battle of Antietam" field study (Sharpsburg, MD: U.S. History Consortium, 2006).
14. Brian Jordan and Brandon Roos, "The Battle of Gaines Mill" field study (Richmond, VA: Making of America Liberty Fellowship, 2008).
15. Ibid.

CHAPTER 5

16. John W. Gordon, *South Carolina in the American Revolution* (Columbia: University of South Carolina Press, 2007), 88.
17. Ibid., 88–89.
18. John A. Stevens, "The Southern Campaign," *Magazine of American History* 5, no. 4 (October 1880).
19. Gordon, *South Carolina in the American Revolution*, 91.
20. Alexander Hamilton to James Duane, September 6, 1780, quoted in Mark M. Boatner III, *Encyclopedia of the American Revolution* (Mechanicsburg, PA: Stackpole, 1994), 415.
21. Gordon, *South Carolina in the American Revolution*, 95.
22. John Buchanan, *The Road to Guilford Courthouse* (New York: John Wiley & Sons, 1997), 181–83.
23. Ibid., 185–86.
24. Davie, *Sketches*, 21–25, as quoted in Buchanan, *Road to Guilford Courthouse*, 188–89.
25. Walter Edgar, *Partisans & Redcoats* (New York: Perennial, 2001), 114–15.

CHAPTER 6

26. Buchanan, *Road to Guilford Courthouse*, 204–7.
27. A Pamphlet by Isaac Shelby, quoted in Ed Southern, *Voices of the American Revolution in the Carolinas* (Winston-Salem, NC: Blair, 2009), 154.
28. Ibid., 155.
29. Wilma Dykeman, *With Fire and Sword: The Battle of Kings Mountain* (Washington, D.C.: U.S. National Park Service, 1975).
30. A Pamphlet by Isaac Shelby, quoted in Southern, *Voices of the American Revolution*, 156–57.
31. Lyman Draper, *Kings Mountain and Its Heroes* (Cincinnati, OH: Peter Thomson, 1881), 200–202.

32. Major Patrick Ferguson, October 1, 1780, quoted in Draper, *Kings Mountain and Its Heroes*, 204.
33. Draper, *Kings Mountain and Its Heroes*, 207.
34. Ibid., 208.
35. Alfred Jones, ed., *The Journal of Alexander Chesney, a South Carolina Loyalist in the American Revolution and After* (Columbus: Ohio State University, 1894), 17.
36. Letter of William McCall to Loyalist McFall, quoted in Draper, *Kings Mountain and Its Heroes*, 210.
37. Jones, *Journal of Alexander Chesney*, 17.
38. Buchanan, *Road to Guilford Courthouse*, 220.
39. Draper, *Kings Mountain and Its Heroes*, 219.
40. A Pamphlet by Isaac Shelby, quoted in Southern, *Voices of the American Revolution*, 158.
41. Draper, *Kings Mountain and Its Heroes*, 223.
42. Buchanan, *Road to Guilford Courthouse*, 222–23.
43. Ibid., 226.
44. Ibid., 227.
45. Ibid.
46. J. David Dameron, *Kings Mountain* (Cambridge, MA: De Capo, 2003), 45.
47. A Pamphlet by Isaac Shelby, quoted in Southern, *Voices of the American Revolution*, 158.
48. Dameron, *Kings Mountain*, 44.

CHAPTER 7

49. Broad River Genealogical Society, *Cleveland County Heritage* (Marceline, MO: Walsworth, 2004), 362.
50. Dameron, *Kings Mountain*, 46.
51. Ibid., 47.
52. Ibid., 48.
53. Dunkerly, *Kings Mountain Walking Tour Guide*, 21.
54. Dameron, *Kings Mountain*, 53.
55. Ibid., 55.
56. Ibid., 56–57.
57. A Pamphlet by Isaac Shelby, quoted in Southern, *Voices of the American Revolution*, 159.
58. Dameron, *Kings Mountain*, 59.

59. Dunkerly, *Kings Mountain Walking Tour Guide*, 20.

60. Dameron, *Kings Mountain*, 59.

61. A Pamphlet by Isaac Shelby, quoted in Southern, *Voices of the American Revolution*, 159.

62. Ibid., 20.

63. Dameron, *Kings Mountain*, 61.

64. Ibid., 61.

65. Jones, *Journal of Alexander Chesney*, 17.

66. Buchanan, *Road to Guilford Courthouse*, 232.

67. Leonard Hice's Pension Application, quoted in Robert Dunkerly, *The Battle of Kings Mountain: Eyewitness Accounts* (Charleston: The History Press, 2007), 250.

68. Samuel Williams's account, *Tennessee Historical Magazine* (Tennessee Historical Society, April 1921), 106.

69. Broad River, *Cleveland County Heritage*, 362.

70. Buchanan, *Road to Guilford Courthouse*, 232.

71. Captain Abraham DePeyster's report to General Cornwallis, quoted in Dunkerly, *Battle of Kings Mountain*, 134.

72. Ensign Robert Campbell's account, quoted in Dunkerly, *Battle of Kings Mountain*, 19.

73. Private James Collins's account, quoted in Dunkerly, *Battle of Kings Mountain*, 34.

74. A Pamphlet by Isaac Shelby, quoted in Southern, *Voices of the American Revolution*, 159.

75. Draper, *Kings Mountain and Its Heroes*, 282.

76. Charles Bowens's pension application quoted in Dunkerly, *Battle of Kings Mountain*, 18.

77. Joseph Hughes's account, quoted in Dunkerly, *Battle of Kings Mountain*, 52.

78. Alexander Chesney's journal, quoted in Dunkerly, *Battle of Kings Mountain*, 132.

CHAPTER 8

79. Jones, *Journal of Alexander Chesney*, 18.

80. Private James Collins's account, quoted in Dunkerly, *Battle of Kings Mountain*, 34.

81. Private James Collins's account, quoted in Dunkerly, *Battle of Kings Mountain*, 35.

82. Lieutenant Anthony Allaire, *Royal Gazette* (New York), February 24, 1781.

83. Jones, *Journal of Alexander Chesney*, 18.

84. Ibid.

85. Sydney Fisher, *The Struggle for American Independence* (Philadelphia, PA: Lippincott, 1908), 361.

86. Allaire, *Royal Gazette* (New York), February 24, 1781.

87. Banastre Tarleton quoted in *Historical Statements Concerning the Battle of Kings Mountain and the Battle of Cowpens, South Carolina* (Washington, D.C.: U.S. Government Printing Office, 1928), 34.

88. Higginbotham, *Daniel Morgan*, 111.

89. Jones, *Journal of Alexander Chesney*, 18.

90. Allaire, *Royal Gazette* (New York), February 24, 1781.

91. Ibid.

92. Ibid.

CHAPTER 9

93. Higginbotham, *Daniel Morgan*, 119–120.

94. Buchanan, *Road to Guilford Courthouse*, 288.

95. Ibid., 290.

96. Greene to Thomas Jefferson, quoted in Theodorus Myers, *Cowpens Papers* (Charleston, SC: News and Courier, 1881), 12–13.

97. Adjutant Williams to Morgan, quoted in Myers, *Cowpens Papers*, 11.

98. Nathanael Greene as quoted in Buchanan, *Road to Guilford Courthouse*, 295.

99. Greene to Morgan, quoted in Myers, *Cowpens Papers*, 9.

100. Ibid.

101. Thomas Fleming, *Cowpens Official National Park Handbook* (Washington, D.C.: U.S. Government Printing Office, 1988), 38.

102. Nathanael Greene to Daniel Morgan, as quoted in Buchanan, *Road to Guilford Courthouse*, 296.

103. Ibid., 298.

104. Ibid., 303–4.

105. Greene to Morgan, quoted in Dennis Conrad, ed., *The Papers of General Nathanael Greene* (Chapel Hill: University of North Carolina Press, 2002), 146.

106. Fleming, *Cowpens Official National Park Handbook*, 32–33.

107. Ibid., 34.

108. Banastre Tarleton, *A History of the Campaigns of 1780 and 1781 in the Southern Provinces of North America* (North Stratford, NH: Ayer Publishers, 1887), 210.

109. Ibid., 209.

110. Charles Cornwallis to Henry Clinton, as quoted in Buchanan, *Road to Guilford Courthouse*, 306–7.

CHAPTER 10

111. Ed Bearss, *Battle of Cowpens* (Johnson City, TN: Overmountain Press, 1996), 5.

112. Ibid.

113. Ibid.

114. Morgan to Greene, quoted in Myers, *Cowpens Papers*, 18.

115. Greene to Morgan, quoted in Myers, *Cowpens Papers*, 19.

116. Tarleton, *History of the Campaigns*, 218.

117. Tarleton to Cornwallis, as quoted in Lawrence Babits, *Cowpens Battlefield: A Walking Guide* (Johnson City, TN: Overmountain Press, 1993), 5.

118. Dennis E. Frye, "The Battle of Antietam" field study, U.S. History Consortium, Sharpsburg, Maryland, 2006.

119. James Williams, *The Life of General Morgan* (New York: Derby & Jackson, 1859), 282.

120. Lawrence Babits, *A Devil of a Whipping* (Chapel Hill: University of North Carolina Press, 1998), 51.

121. Ibid., 52.

122. Ibid., 52–53.

123. Tarleton, *History of the Campaigns*, 220.

124. Thomas Young's memoirs, quoted in Southern, *Voices of the American Revolution*, 181.

125. Tarleton, *History of the Campaigns*, 220.

126. Jones, *Journal of Alexander Chesney*, 21.

127. Bernhard Uhlendorf, ed., *Confidential Letters and Journals 1776–1784 of Adjutant General Major Baurmiester of the Hessian Forces* (New Brunswick, NJ: Rutgers University Press, 1957), 414.

128. Tarleton, *History of the Campaigns*, 221.

129. John Eager Howard, as quoted in Babits, *A Devil of a Whipping*, 53.

130. Lieutenant Colonel Jon Moncure, *The Cowpens Staff Ride and Battlefield Tour* (Fort Leavenworth, KS: Combat Studies Institute, 1996), 46.

131. Moncure, *Cowpens Staff Ride*, 45.

132. Daniel Morgan, as quoted in Moncure, *Cowpens Staff Ride*, 46.
133. Fleming, *Cowpens Official National Park Handbook*, 45.

CHAPTER 11

134. Morgan to Greene, quoted in Myers, *Cowpens Papers*, 24.
135. Thomas Young's memoirs, quoted in Southern, *Voices of the American Revolution*, 181.
136. Ibid., 181–82.
137. Burke Davis, *The Cowpens-Guilford Courthouse Campaign* (Philadelphia: University of Pennsylvania Press, 1962), 22.
138. Thomas Young's memoirs, quoted in Southern, *Voices of the American Revolution*, 182.
139. James Collins, as quoted in Henry S. Commager and Richard B. Morris, eds., *The Spirit of 'Seventy-Six*, vol. II (Indianapolis, IN: Bobbs-Merrill Company, 1968), 1156.
140. James Williams, *The Life of General Morgan* (New York: Derby & Jackson, 1859), 299.
141. Thomas Young's memoirs, quoted in Southern, *Voices of the American Revolution*, 182.
142. Uhlendorf, *Confidential Letters and Journals*, 414.
143. Moncure, *Cowpens Staff Ride*, 52.
144. Daniel Morgan, as quoted by Thomas Young's memoirs, quoted in Southern, *Voices of the American Revolution*, 182.
145. Thomas Young's memoirs, quoted in Southern, *Voices of the American Revolution*, 183.
146. Moncure, *Cowpens Staff Ride*, 56.
147. Thomas Young's memoirs, quoted in Southern, *Voices of the American Revolution*, 183.
148. James Collins, as quoted in Davis, *Cowpens-Guilford Courthouse Campaign*, 33.
149. Ibid.
150. Tarleton, *History of the Campaigns*, 223.
151. Moncure, *Cowpens Staff Ride*, 58.
152. Ibid.
153. Burke, *Cowpens-Guilford Courthouse Campaign*, 35.
154. John Eager Howard, as quoted in Commager and Morris, *Spirit of 'Seventy-Six*, 1157.
155. Ibid.

156. Moncure, *Cowpens Staff Ride*, 60.
157. William Washington, as quoted in Davis, *Cowpens-Guilford Courthouse Campaign*, 36.
158. Thomas Young's memoirs, quoted in Southern, *Voices of the American Revolution*, 184.
159. James Collins, as quoted in William Cumming and Hugh Rankin, *The Fate of a Nation* (London: Phaidon, 1975), 296.
160. James Collins, as quoted in Commager and Morris, *Spirit of 'Seventy-Six*, 1156.
161. Babits, *A Devil of a Whipping*, 153; Moncure, *Cowpens Staff Ride*, 60.
162. Tarleton, *History of the Campaigns*, 223.
163. Ibid.
164. Moncure, *Cowpens Staff Ride*, 62.
165. Tarleton, *History of the Campaigns*, 223.
166. James Graham, *The Life of General Daniel Morgan* (New York: Derby & Jackson, 1859), 306.
167. Fleming, *Cowpens Official National Park Handbook*, 76.
168. Moncure, *Cowpens Staff Ride*, 62.
169. Graham, *Life of General Daniel Morgan*, 306–7.
170. Ibid., 305.
171. Fleming, *Cowpens Official National Park Handbook*, 70.
172. Morgan to Greene, quoted in Myers, *Cowpens Papers*, 26.
173. Ibid.
174. Tarleton, *History of the Campaigns*, 224.
175. Ibid.
176. Ibid.
177. Morgan to Greene, quoted in Myers, *Cowpens Papers*, 26.

CHAPTER 12

178. Higginbotham, *Daniel Morgan*, 144.
179. Ibid.
180. Davis, *Cowpens-Guilford Courthouse Campaign*, 45.
181. Tarleton to Morgan, quoted in Myers, *Cowpens Papers*, 29.
182. Tarleton, *History of the Campaigns*, 221.
183. Jones, *Journal of Alexander Chesney*, 22.
184. Tarleton, *History of the Campaigns*, 221.
185. Don Hagist, ed., *A Soldier's Story: Roger Lamb's Narrative of the American Revolution* (London: Ballindoch, 2004), 80.
186. Ibid.

Chapter 13

187. Graham, *Life of General Daniel Morgan*, 348.
188. Ibid., 350.
189. Ibid., 350–51.
190. Daniel Morgan to Nathanael Greene, as quoted in Graham, *Life of General Daniel Morgan*, 355.
191. Nathanael Greene to Daniel Morgan, as quoted in Graham, *Life of General Daniel Morgan*, 358.

Chapter 14

192. Davidson to Morgan, quoted in Myers, *Cowpens Papers*, 32.
193. Williams to Morgan, quoted in Myers, *Cowpens Papers*, 33.
194. Jones, *Journal of Alexander Chesney*, 23.
195. Williams to Morgan, quoted in Myers, *Cowpens Papers*, 33.
196. Rutledge to Morgan, quoted in Myers, *Cowpens Papers*, 34.

BIBLIOGRAPHY

Babits, Lawrence. *Cowpens Battlefield: A Walking Guide.* Johnson City, TN: Overmountain Press, 1993.

——. *A Devil of a Whipping.* Chapel Hill: UNC Press, 1998.

Bearss, Ed. *Battle of Cowpens.* Johnson City, TN: Overmountain Press, 1996.

Boatner, Mark M., III. *Encyclopedia of the American Revolution.* Mechanicsburg, PA: Stackpole, 1994.

Broad River Genealogical Society. *Cleveland County Heritage.* Marceline, MO: Walsworth, 2004.

Buchanan, John. *The Road to Guilford Courthouse.* New York: John Wiley & Sons, 1997.

Commager Henry S. and Morris Richard B., eds. *The Spirit of 'Seventy-Six.* Volume II. Indianapolis, IN: Bobbs-Merrill Company, 1968.

Conrad, Dennis, ed. *The Papers of General Nathanael Greene.* Chapel Hill: University of North Carolina Press, 2002.

Cumming, William, and Hugh Rankin. *The Fate of a Nation.* London: Phaidon, 1975.

Dameron, J. David. *Kings Mountain.* Cambridge, MA: Da Capo, 2003.

Davis, Burke. *The Cowpens-Guilford Courthouse Campaign.* Philadelphia: University of Pennsylvania Press, 1962.

Draper, Lyman. *Kings Mountain and Its Heroes.* Cincinnati, OH: Peter Thomson, 1881.

Dunkerly, Robert. *The Battle of Kings Mountain: Eyewitness Accounts.* Charleston, SC: The History Press, 2007.

——. *Kings Mountain Walking Tour Guide.* Pittsburgh, PA: Dorrance, 2003.

Dykeman, Wilma. *With Fire and Sword: The Battle of Kings Mountain.* Washington, D.C.: National Park Service, 1975.

Edgar, Walter. *Partisans & Redcoats.* New York: Harper-Collins, 2003.

Fisher, Sydney. *The Struggle for American Independence.* Philadelphia, PA: Lippincott, 1908.

Fleming, Thomas. *Cowpens Official National Park Handbook.* Washington, D.C.: U.S. Government Printing Office, 1988.

Gilmore Simms, William. *The Scout.* Chicago: Donohue Hennenberry & Co., 1890.

Gordon, John W. *South Carolina in the American Revolution.* Columbia: University of South Carolina Press, 2007.

Hagist, Don, ed. *A Soldier's Story: Roger Lamb's Narrative of the American Revolution.* London: Ballindoch, 2004.

Higginbotham, Don. *Daniel Morgan Revolutionary Rifleman.* Chapel Hill: University of North Carolina Press, 1961.

Jones, Alfred, ed. *The Journal of Alexander Chesney, a South Carolina Loyalist in the American Revolution and After.* Columbus: Ohio State University, 1894.

Moncure, Jon, Lieutenant Colonel. *The Cowpens Staff Ride and Battlefield Tour.* Fort Leavenworth, KS: Combat Studies Institute, 1996.

Myers, Theodorus. *Cowpens Papers.* Charleston, SC: News and Courier, 1881.

Southern, Ed. *Voices of the American Revolution in the Carolinas.* Winston-Salem, NC: Blair, 2009.

Tarleton, Banastre. *A History of the Campaigns of 1780 and 1781 in the Southern Provinces of North America.* North Stratford: Ayer Publishers, 1887.

Uhlendorf, Bernhard, ed. *Confidential Letters and Journals 1776–1784 of Adjutant General Major Baurmiester of the Hessian Forces.* New Brunswick, NJ: Rutgers University Press, 1957.

U.S. Government Printing Office. *Historical Statements Concerning the Battle of Kings Mountain and the Battle of Cowpens, South Carolina.* Washington, D.C.: U.S. Government Printing Office, 1928.

Williams, James. *The Life of General Morgan.* New York: Derby & Jackson, 1859.

www.ingramcontent.com/pod-product-compliance
Lightning Source LLC
Chambersburg PA
CBHW060802100426
42813CB00004B/921